Praise for

Saturday Night, Sunday Morning

"PJ Morton is a once-in-a-generation talent and someone who has changed the course of my life for the better. Getting to understand more of what influenced him to become the genre-melding artist, dedicated family man, and forward-thinking businessperson that he is today was such a treat. He combined his passion and understanding of R & B *and* gospel into a sound all his own. If you love music like I do, you'll love *Saturday Night, Sunday Morning.*"

—Joanna "JoJo" Levesque, Grammy Award–winning singer and songwriter

"In his compelling new book, *Saturday Night, Sunday Morning*, PJ Morton invites us into the depths of his personal journey—a soulful exploration of struggle, discovery, and the unwavering commitment to his faith and music.

"Morton's narrative unfolds with raw honesty as he navigates the delicate balance between personal boundaries and his artistic voice. Through his experiences, he illuminates the path for countless gifted individuals who, like him, began their journey in the sanctuary of church walls.

"What sets PJ apart is his resolute dedication to using his musical gift to transcend barriers and touch the hearts of people worldwide. In his lyrical prose, he not only shares his own triumphs and trials but also offers a profound road map for others seeking to harness their talents for a higher purpose.

"'Singing the universal language of love,' PJ beautifully captures the essence of his music—a testament to his unwavering faith and the transformative power of art. His story resonates with anyone who has wrestled with the intersection of passion and belief, ultimately finding harmony in their pursuit.

"*Saturday Night, Sunday Morning* is not just a memoir but a testament to the enduring power of faith, love, and the unbreakable spirit of an artist whose voice transcends boundaries. PJ's journey is an inspiration—an invitation to embrace one's gifts fully and use them to illuminate the world."

—Bishop Joseph Warren Walker III, international presiding bishop, Full Gospel Baptist Church Fellowship, senior pastor, Mount Zion Nashville

Saturday Night Sunday Morning

Saturday Night Sunday Morning

Staying True to Myself from the Pews to the Stage

PJ MORTON

WORTHY
PUBLISHING

New York • Nashville

Worthy

Hachette Book Group

1290 Avenue of the Americas, New York, NY 10104

worthypublishing.com

@WorthyPub

First edition: November 2024

Worthy is a division of Hachette Book Group, Inc. The Worthy name and logo are registered trademarks of Hachette Book Group, Inc.

The publisher is not responsible for websites (or their content) that are not owned by the publisher.

Worthy Books may be purchased in bulk for business, educational, or promotional use. For information, please contact your local bookseller or the Hachette Book Group Special Markets Department at special.markets@hbgusa.com.

Print book interior design by Bart Dawson.

Library of Congress Cataloging-in-Publication Data

Names: Morton, P. J., 1981– author.

Title: Saturday night, Sunday morning : staying true to myself from the pews to the stage / PJ Morton.

Description: First edition. | New York : Worthy Books, 2024.

Identifiers: LCCN 2024023820 | ISBN 9781546006657 (hardcover) | ISBN 9781546006671 (ebook)

Subjects: LCSH: Morton, P. J., 1981– | Singers—United States—Biography. | Keyboard players—United States—Biography. | Rhythm and blues musicians—United States—Biography. | Maroon 5 (Musical group) | LCGFT: Autobiographies.

Classification: LCC ML420.M63515 A3 2024 | DDC 782.421644092 [B]—dc23/eng/20240524

LC record available at https://lccn.loc.gov/2024023820

ISBNs: 9781546006657 (hardcover), 9781546006671 (ebook)

Printed in the United States of America

LSC-C

Printing 1, 2024

To my dad—to the one who taught me how to be a man. How to be a father. How to have vision and dream big. The one who taught me to not just see it but to work hard to make it happen. The one who taught me to be kind to people.

I love you, Dad. Thank you.

Contents

Contents

Encore

Foreword

For thirty-five years now I've been hosting a show on TNT called *Inside the NBA*, sharing the screen with Charles Barkley, Shaquille O'Neal, and Kenny Smith. A centerpiece of our coverage every season is the NBA's All-Star Weekend, and for a couple of decades now, one of the events of that weekend is something I've been honored to emcee. It's called the Legends Brunch, where some of the game's brightest stars are saluted. Others, who have passed in the previous year, are likewise remembered in what is always a sobering, heartfelt few minutes.

That's how I first met PJ Morton.

New Orleans was hosting All-Star Weekend in 2017. The producer of the Legends Brunch, George DeFotis, and I were going over the run of show a couple of hours beforehand. When we got to the "In Memoriam" portion of the rundown, he said, "PJ Morton will be singing as we show images of those we've lost in the past year." I'll be honest here. I didn't know who PJ was, but George said, "He plays keyboards for Maroon 5." Now, look, I know who Maroon 5 is. In fact, I had taken my daughter Carmen to one of their concerts outside Atlanta. (Every now and then I have the capability of being a cool dad, and going to a Maroon 5 show, at least in my estimation, qualified.) I just didn't know the band members.

But after what I heard that day in New Orleans when PJ took the stage, I knew I would never forget him. I introduced the segment and glanced to my right, where a spotlight in the darkened ballroom shone on PJ at his keyboard. As massive video screens displayed photos and archive footage of former NBA players, he delivered an absolutely heartrending yet uplifting version of Donnie Hathaway's "A Song for You." It was perfect, from first note to last. A thousand or so NBA fans sat in reverential silence, riveted. I took the stage after that performance, speechless—which is never a good thing to be when you're expected to introduce the next segment. I managed to do that, and then rushed backstage, hoping to catch PJ before he left, just to let him know how powerful his performance had been. We had a chance to speak for a few minutes and take a quick photo.

A few months later, we arranged for PJ and his band to come to the TNT studios on a game night, where he rocked the joint with "Sticking to My Guns," and the following December, as part of our Christmas show on TNT, he returned to provide some holiday flavor. Again he delivered in a way that was simply good for your soul. The man has a gift.

I got hooked on his solo efforts—especially the album *Gumbo*, which became a fixture on my playlists. Fast-forward a couple of years, and there came an occasion in Atlanta that will remain incredibly special for me and my wife. We had just lost one of our children, Michael. We had adopted him from Romania in the early nineties. Born with muscular dystrophy, he far outlived expectations—a remarkable thirty-three years. It was only a few months after Michael died in October 2021 that PJ and his outstanding right-hand man, Wade Jordan, reached out, as they often did, to alert me to the fact that PJ would be playing in Atlanta. My wife, Cheryl, and I made our way to City Winery on a Sunday night and spent some time pre-show talking to PJ. I had told Cheryl all about him...how she needed to meet him...how he was cool and humble and talented—all those things her husband had yet to master. And we shared with PJ Michael's story, about the grief that was still so fresh and how a night out like this would give us a much-needed break.

The show was magical.

As I said, the man has a gift.

And then it happened.

As he introduced the song "Everything's Gonna Be Alright," he looked toward our table and spoke to us. He said he understood what was going on in our lives and hoped that we would take comfort in the fact that in time everything was gonna be all right. We will never forget that act of kindness, that display of empathy. I'll never forget the total stranger at our table who reached out and took Cheryl's hand in hers. I tear up now just writing this, almost as much as I did when listening that night and singing along with everyone else.

Over the last few years, it has given me such joy to remain in contact with PJ, to send congratulatory texts his way for his solo accomplishments—the string of multiple Grammy awards. Here's a man—the son of a preacher—who humbly accepts the platitudes and shares the Gospel in an effortless and gracious way. He's never forgotten his roots and has always had this air of gratitude about him. It's refreshing to experience. It has been an honor to call him a friend. *Saturday Night, Sunday Morning* tells the story of what happens at the intersection of talent, determination, and

Divine intervention. I know you'll find wisdom in the pages that follow.

Because, as I've said, the man has a gift.

Ernie Johnson Jr.,
host of *Inside the NBA*,
author of *Unscripted: The Unpredictable Moments
That Make Life Extraordinary*

Saturday Night Sunday Morning

Prologue

"Just play something, Paul."

It was 1996, and I was fifteen years old. I was in the front room of my parents' house on Wright Road in New Orleans East, seated at our baby grand piano. Sitting next to me on the bench, close enough that I could smell his aftershave, was Mr. Alphonse, my piano teacher. He was an older Black man with gray hair, a gray mustache, and glasses—a sweet man and a kind, patient teacher.

My mom, Dr. Debra Brown Morton, loved classical piano and wanted all her children to learn to play the traditional way. My dad, Bishop Paul S. Morton Sr., had a different perspective. He was from a musical family and had spent his whole life in and around music, and everyone he knew who played piano had learned to play by ear. But he was busy, so he let my mom do things her way. That meant piano lessons.

My sister Jasmine, who's four years older than me, went first, taking lessons with a teacher named Mr. Burns. When I turned ten years old, it was my turn. I had been teaching myself to play by ear by playing the songs I heard on TV and the radio, but Mr. Burns wanted me to play scales. I thought that was a waste of time, because the scales were so much more basic than what I was already playing. But I was an obedient, respectful child, so I did my best.

Prologue

When you start off in piano lessons, you read numbers instead of notes, and at first I really tried to learn the patterns by the numbers. Still, I ended up playing the pieces by ear because learning them that way was so much easier and faster. But Mr. Burns wasn't fooled. He would snap, "Paul, you're not reading the music. You're playing extra stuff that's not even there." I couldn't help it! I didn't want to learn the traditional way. A few more weeks and my mom decided that maybe I wasn't ready for piano lessons yet.

Now, five years later, I was trying again with Mr. Alphonse. My playing was a lot more advanced by this time, because I had been playing on my own a lot. When I was twelve, I started a band, Christians Combined, to play at my father's church, and three years of gigs and rehearsals had really helped me develop my technique and ear. But for my mom's sake, I still tried to learn the old-fashioned way.

I had four or five lessons with Mr. Alphonse. He would sit right next to me and have me play a pattern, watching my fingers move up and down the keys. Then he would say, "Do it again." I would repeat the pattern, and he would say, "Do it again."

Then came that day when he asked me to just play something. I looked at him, confused. Gently, he said, "Just play whatever you want to play." So I played something that I made up on the spot. I don't even remember what it was, just a series of chords and notes.

When I had finished playing, Mr. Alphonse was smiling. Then he said the words that would set the course of my life: "Paul, what you have is something I can't teach people. I don't know if you really need lessons. You've got the gift." For a long time, I had known I could do things at the piano that other people couldn't. I could hear a song once and just play it, naturally, without thinking about it. But no one outside my family had ever told me that I had a gift. It wasn't a long conversation, but that was the moment I decided to quit piano lessons and put all my energy into playing my way.

I never did learn to read music. I used to think, *Man, if I could read* and *have this natural ear, I could be dangerous.* But you know who can't read music? Stevie Wonder and Paul McCartney. You know who couldn't read music? Prince and Michael Jackson. I think I've done all right.

~

Ventura Park, Portland, Oregon, July 9, 2023.

It was a warm, dry summer afternoon, and my band and I were having a fantastic time entertaining a joyful crowd at the second annual East Portland Summer Arts Festival, with the theme "Celebrating Black Excellence." The summer-brown grass of the park was covered with thousands of people on blankets and in folding chairs, kids on the swings, all here to see me, a preacher's kid.

I was surrounded by a group of friends—family, really—who had been playing and singing with me on the road for years, sometimes decades. Pressed up against the stage barriers was a line of people—white, Black, Hispanic, men, women—who had been on their feet dancing for the entire show, singing along, lost in the music. Behind them, curving in a semicircle throughout the park, thousands more were dancing, clapping, and singing along with my music. *My music.* I was the headliner, the reason all these people were there.

The band and I would close out the festival with my Grammy-winning version of "How Deep Is Your Love," spend time playing spades, relaxing, eating, clowning, and enjoying each other like we always did, then I would fly home for a few days to film a segment for BET. A few weeks later, I would fly out to Las Vegas to hook up with the guys from Maroon 5 and resume our residency at the Park MGM.

~

Those two episodes are the bookends of my life, and sometimes, it's still hard to believe how much has changed for me, and just as hard to believe how little has changed. On the one hand, I'm composing for Disney and for Hollywood, touring Africa, and writing a memoir. On the other, I'm still a preacher's kid steeped in gospel traditions and living in New Orleans, only now I live there with my wife and three children, one of whom is in college.

Somewhere in the middle, I'm still doing what I've done since I was a boy of fourteen, fascinated by Stevie Wonder and wanting to make my dad proud: playing the piano the way Mr. Alphonse gave me permission to play it, making the music I love with the people I love, and doing it on my own terms. I've come full circle, cracked the code, and figured out how to be independent in a world of compromise.

In between Mr. Alphonse at the piano and that warm, appreciative crowd in the Pacific Northwest, a great deal happened to shape the person I've become, more than I could ever put in this book. But looking back, I've noticed a pattern that's pretty revealing. I'm a natural people pleaser, but every time in my life that I've set aside my vision of what makes me happy and fulfilled in order to do what I thought someone else wanted, it's been the wrong decision.

Prologue

That's how I ended up feeling misunderstood and alone as a young man, trying to convince myself to follow the path of a gospel musician. I started down that road because I thought it was what my dad wanted. I even came within inches of launching a can't-miss gospel group before backtracking in a panic. Ironically, all my dad ever wanted was for me to be myself.

That's how I wound up—after years of making independent records I loved, touring with friends, and playing for rooms of fans who sang along with every lyric—sitting in a series of humiliating, demoralizing meetings with record executives who told me they loved everything about my music except for what they wanted to change, which was everything. It's how I burned out so badly on the music business that I told my worried wife, Kortni, "I'm done," put my tail between my legs, and moved back to New Orleans, ready to turn my back on my music career and run a sneaker store.

Every time I failed to listen to my authentic artist's voice and trust my instincts, I ended up compromising, chasing things that didn't matter—commercial hits, popular acclaim, awards—and wondering why I was miserable.

On the other hand, whenever I've disregarded outside influences, followed my instincts, and trusted my vision, incredible things have come my way without my even trying. Because I had faith in my vision, I got a call one day to audition for Maroon 5 and became part of not only one of the biggest bands in the world, but a group of guys I love like brothers.

Because I listened to the instincts that told me to make the music that lit me up and not care what anyone else thought of it, I started writing more than love songs and ended up with my album

Gumbo, which led to a groundbreaking live record, a shocking Grammy win (the first of five, if you can believe it), and the resurrection of a career I thought was over. In 2022, the Walt Disney Company reached out to me because of my music and my New Orleans roots and offered me one of my dream jobs: writing the theme song for a new theme park ride! I'm the first Black artist to write a song for an attraction at Walt Disney World and Disneyland, which is an incredible honor.

Because I followed my heart, I took my closest friends on an African adventure that not only produced thrilling live performances and a new album but opened my eyes to a continent and a people that felt like coming home.

And by stubbornly doing things my own independent way and building a catalog of respected albums and songs, I became a hero and a mentor to a whole new generation of young, up-and-coming musicians.

Even that day at the piano with my teacher was a contest of wills. Would I do what I knew was right for me, or would I conform to what other people thought was right for me? I'll never know if that advice from Mr. Alphonse tipped the balance toward independence, but I suspect that it did.

Whatever the reason, following my heart and trusting my voice as an artist has always been the surest way to success for me. And I think there's a lesson in that. See, artists aren't meant to compromise; that's not why we're here. Artists challenge authority, ask hard questions, and bring comfort and hope in dark times. We can't do that if we're more concerned about ticket sales and charting hits than telling our truth.

I lost myself in the lie for a while, and when I found my way out again, I saw the truth. The only way to happiness and lasting success is to listen to your own voice, trust yourself, and never compromise on your vision. To be fair, when you go into the world that way, people will misunderstand you. They'll insist, for your own good, that you have to change everything or you'll get nowhere. Even if you stick to your guns and have some success, doors will be slammed in your face because you don't fit the model.

Eventually, if you push back long enough, you'll be burned out. Ironically, if you enjoy commercial success and start to think it's the most important thing in life, you'll burn out, too. Because it's not. If I've learned anything, it's that success is a road that, if you walk it right, brings you back to what you love most. For me, that's those lifelong friends I was playing music with in Portland. It's my Kortni and my kids (did I mention one of them is in college?). It's the city where I was born and that I've only recently come to see with fresh eyes.

I walked that road, and I didn't even know I was on it. The trouble with that is that you never know when you're close to a breakthrough. It could be around the next corner. It was for me, and if you want to walk with me for a while, I'll show you.

PJ Morton
New Orleans, Louisiana
March 2024

Saturday Night Sunday Morning

Part One

~

Warm-Up

Chapter One

First Began

You can't appreciate my story unless you understand the things that influenced me the most. The first one was, of course, my family.

My dad was born and raised in Windsor, Ontario, Canada, across the Ambassador Bridge from Detroit, and was the youngest of four sons (along with five daughters) born to Clarence Leslie Morton Sr. and his wife, Matilda Elizabeth Morton. I never met my grandfather, who everyone knew as "CL," because he died when my dad was twelve, but he was a legend in the Christian community. He founded the Canadian and International Churches of God in Christ (COGIC, an important part of the Pentecostal tradition) in Windsor and Detroit and led churches in two countries: Mount Zion Full Gospel Church in Windsor, and Mt. Zion Tabernacle on Woodward Avenue in Detroit. At that time, in the 1950s, leading two congregations at the same time was cutting-edge.

My dad's childhood was all about church. He wasn't allowed to play sports as a kid, and the only music any of the kids could listen to was church music. My grandfather's churches were a big deal, and so was his radio ministry. He would lead these famous Sunday night services that were carried on the radio in both countries. He would come on the air and preach sermons like "Where Is the Sacrifice?" with all the fire and praise you can imagine. It was like the *Hour of Power*, and everybody on both sides of the border would tune in to hear this eloquent man talk about the Lord and the Word.

My grandfather died in 1962. His oldest son, my uncle Clarence Jr., who was only twenty, became one of the youngest bishops in the country and took over the ministry at Mount Zion Church in Windsor. He also took over the responsibility of raising my dad and training him in the family business, teaching him how to preach and write his first message. My dad really looked up to Uncle Clarence, who died in 2020 and was probably one of the first people in Detroit to pass away from COVID-19.

Early on, my family was heavily involved in music. My uncle Jimmy, the second oldest son, played keys and played for the Baptist minister CL Franklin, Aretha Franklin's father, at Franklin's New Bethel Baptist Church in Detroit. I've heard that Uncle Jimmy even played on some Motown records.

Meanwhile, my dad was becoming well known for his choir directing. He and some of his siblings even formed a vocal group, The Mortons. They were all very musical, and they became close with many of the big musical families of the time, including the Clark Sisters, the top-selling female gospel group in history, whose mother, Dr. Mattie Moss Clark, was the International Minister of Music for the Church of God in Christ. They also got to know the Winans family, one of the leading families in gospel music, because their grandfather had been close to my grandfather. Our families have stayed close through all these years, so gospel music has been a part of my heritage since long before I was born.

In 1972, my dad was preaching at a revival in Cleveland when he was robbed of everything he owned. Right after that, he heard God's voice telling him to move to New Orleans. Once, he told me that it had to be God's voice, because he didn't know anybody in New Orleans and had no reason to go there. He was just twenty-two, but he did what God asked and moved, arriving in the city with no family and knowing no one. But he just happened to move into a place right down the street from what was then called Greater St. Stephen Missionary Baptist Church.

My mother's grandmother was one of the founders of Greater St. Stephen, and when my dad went there, he met my mom, who was just a young girl at the time. He became the youth pastor, and when Reverend Percy Simpson, pastor of Greater St. Stephen, died in a car accident in 1974, my father became senior pastor.

Two years later, my dad proposed to my mother, although she likes to say that he proposed twice, while he insists quite sincerely that the first proposal was just a test, because he wasn't really ready to get married. "I have to always be sure," he said in a documentary about his church produced by Tyler Perry, a longtime family friend. "You don't make a move and be turned down."

Finally, he proposed for real, my mom accepted, and they got married and began building and growing the church according to their shared vision.

~

I think I inherited my dad's work ethic, because when I was younger, he worked hard. He was always an in-demand speaker, so when he wasn't at home in New Orleans growing the church, he was on the road, preaching at churches and revivals around the country. That meant he was away from home about one hundred days a year. But when he was home, we were always together.

Even though he was away a lot, I never felt that my dad neglected us. I've seen fathers who come home from work every night, ignore their kids, and just sit in front of the TV or surf the Internet. They're there, but they're not there, you know? That was never my dad. Even though he didn't have anyone to teach him because his father died so young, he knew what it meant to be a good father. When he was home, he always gave us his complete attention, and was intentional about making sure we spent time together—especially that we ate dinner together. While we would be just fine doing our own things in different parts of the house, he knew it was important for us to share space and have conversation, whether we were eating or playing a game, or he was reading to us.

While my dad is serious and intense, my mom is his perfect opposite number. She's got style, flair, and imagination. She's the first person who made me care about fashion. I remember walking into her room when I was a kid and the TV would be tuned to the E! Entertainment Network, and Mom would be watching fashion-related programming. If she hadn't married my father and become a preacher's wife, I think she would've gone to fashion school in New York and lived a whole different life. Since she didn't do that, she put her love of style into the way she dressed. Even now, as an older lady, my mom is very fly. My younger friends will see my mom, who's in her seventies, and say, "Yo, your mom can dress!"

She's a New Orleans girl who was born in the Magnolia Projects, but she absorbed a lot of culture from the people around her. Somehow, she always knew there was more for her than New Orleans. For example, classical music isn't exactly a thing in Black culture, but she loves it, and she would have it playing when she picked us up from school. I don't know anybody who listens to classical on the radio, but my mom does.

She's also a dreamer. She was always full of ideas when I was a kid. My dad was the visionary, but she was the one saying, "Why don't we maybe try this?" She had a way of adding flavor and a beautiful edge to my father's ideas. Our house reflected her sense of style. It was a good-size five-bedroom house, and she always decorated it beautifully with vivid patterns and colors. She was also into architecture. When we would go on vacations in places like Florida, she would take me to Miami to see the art deco buildings, including the home of Gianni Versace, the fashion designer.

My mom stayed at home with us until my younger sister started kindergarten. Taking care of kids is a full-time job, but all of a sudden hers were gone, so she got a job as a travel agent. She wasn't going to sit around and be bored, so she did something about it. That's what my mom is like.

~

My older sister, Jasmine (whom I call Jay), is four years older than me. She's a great big sister and a classic firstborn child, which means she's a total Goody Two-shoes. She was the perfect little kid who did everything her parents said. It was a challenge for me to keep up that same kind of facade, but that's really who Jay is. She's a perfectionist who believes in following the rules.

When we were kids, she was also the perfect companion. I looked up to her and felt lucky that she let me into her world. We would go on these bike rides that felt to me like we had traveled for thirty miles, but when I looked around, we had gone only a few blocks. We'd find empty lots or creek beds, gather sticks and rocks like they were pirate treasures, and then trade them with one another until it started to get dark and we had to pedal home.

Jasmine was always super talented. She's a great singer, and when I was a kid, she played classical piano, too. We went to her recitals, and I remember thinking, *Man, my sister's really dope.* I thought she could teach me one day. But once I started playing, she gave it up, because she was only playing to please our parents. One pianist in the family was enough to satisfy everybody. She would watch me play without looking at any music and ask, "How do you do this? How did you know how to play that? Who told you how to play that?"

I'd say, "I don't know. I just know how to play it," which was true.

Then there's my younger sister, Christiann. If I'm being honest, I don't think she was planned. She's six years younger than me, and ten years younger than Jasmine, so I think my parents were done. Then…surprise! But she was literally my baby, because I took care of her. My mom and dad wrote a lullaby that I would sing to her when we were playing: *Christiann Xani, so sweet to me, Christiann Xani, sweet as can be.* We became tight in a different way than I was with Jasmine.

I left for college when Christy was only twelve, so I missed out on a lot of her life. For a few years, she was more like an only child, living with my mom and dad in the big house they bought after I left for Morehouse. But we're super close now. She and her kids are over at my house all the time, and I'm as tight with my nephews and my nieces as she and I could have been if we'd been closer in age.

~

My dad has a big extended family, but most of them lived in other cities so we'd usually only see them at Christmas. Those Christmases were noisy, big, and festive. My aunts and uncles (my father's siblings) would travel down to New Orleans from Detroit, where most of them lived, and everybody would gather at our house for a huge Christmas party.

Back then, we had church services on Christmas morning, so my dad always woke us up at 6:00 a.m. and filmed us with a camcorder. I remember waking up groggy and seeing him with the camera in my face. *Thanks, Dad.* I was sleepy, but I was more excited about my gifts. I got to open one gift before church, and then I opened the rest after church. We'd have Christmas service and then come back to the house to open gifts and start watching impatiently out the windows for cars we knew would come up Wright Road.

My sisters and I couldn't wait for all our cousins, aunts, and uncles to arrive. Christmas was always an epic event, and the turnout at my parents' house was always huge. There would be my uncle Jimmy, plus Jason, Jim, and Kim, his kids. There'd be my aunt Nancy and her sons Billy, Bobby, and Darnell (who all lived with us at one time or another). There was my aunt Gwen, who was my dad's executive assistant for many years and worked for the church, and my dad's sister, my aunt Jackie.

My cousins are close to me in age, so when they were here, it was like a vacation. Whatever toys I had, whatever new things I got for Christmas, we were playing on them. I always had a video game system: Nintendo, then Genesis and PlayStation. Then I got into music, so we played keyboard. My cousins and I were inseparable. Jason would tell me about the cool things happening in Atlanta, and Darnell would tell me what was happening in Detroit. I would cry every time they left, because they were like my brothers.

Aunt Nancy was the one always encouraging me to play music. There are videos of her shouting, "Whoo, go ahead!" when I was so little, I could barely play two keys on the piano at the same time. Darnell and Kim were singers, too. Darnell was kind of a prodigy, and Kim eventually sang for Mary J. Blige as a background singer. Then there were my uncle Clarence's kids, CL and Natalie, who eventually moved down to New Orleans. Natalie was married for a short time to Joey Britton, an organ player who ended up becoming my mentor. That was the gist of our big family.

Music has always been a big part of Christmas for us, so when everybody finally arrived at our house, it was time to start singing Christmas carols. We'd make them super gospel, super soulful, and we do the same thing today. One year, Joey Britton was there, and so was my cousin DeeDee, who married my best friend's brother, a member of the gospel group Men of Standard. They made our music even better. But no matter what songs we sang on Christmas, we always had to end with "Silent Night." My dad is a creature of habit, and late in the evening, he'd shush everybody and say, "All right, come on, family, let's do 'Silent Night.'" We would harmonize together and end the night on "...sleep in heavenly peace."

One year, we decided to sing "The Twelve Days of Christmas," but the best part of that song was that our family friend Kim, who can't sing at all, sang her part at the top of her lungs. She was horrible, and when we laughed at her, she laughed right back. Each time we went through the song, a different person would sing a long, drawn-out "Five golden rings…!" and each time it got longer and more dramatic. At the end, we all gave each other a standing ovation.

Meanwhile, my grandmother and my mom were cooking in the background: turkey, ham, dressing, macaroni, yams, and we always had gumbo. The smell of the roasting turkey and the yams made my mouth water. My grandmother worked as a chef at Commander's Palace, a famous creole restaurant, so she knew her way around a kitchen. Those were good times, the best times.

Those Christmas gatherings were the one time my dad would relax and let his hair down. He was comfortable and surrounded by the people who knew him before he was the bishop. He could just be himself.

~

I grew up in New Orleans East, which was a newish suburb back in 1981 when I was born. I lived in the same house on Wright Road from the time I was one year old until I went off to Atlanta to attend Morehouse College in 1999. I don't remember the house we lived in for the first year of my life, other than a vague memory of my dad setting me on top of the refrigerator as part of a game we would play. (I'm probably going to get him in trouble writing this, because I don't think my mom ever knew about that.)

New Orleans East was a sprawling neighborhood wedged between Lake Pontchartrain to the north and Lake Borgne to the southeast, with the Bayou Sauvage Urban National Wildlife Refuge due east. We lived in a big house with a piano in the front room, and I started banging on that piano when I was about eight years old. Back then, most boys my age turned on the television as soon as they got home from school to watch cartoons or the *ABC Afterschool Special*, but not me. I would drop my bag and head straight for that piano to try and play the songs my father and the band had performed in church on Sunday.

Growing up in New Orleans, I also got to enjoy things I would never have seen if I'd been born in any other city. One of my favorite memories from those years was going to church on "Super Sundays." Those were the Sundays after Mardi Gras season started, when there would be "second line" parades that would block off the streets.

If you don't know New Orleans, I need to explain. You probably know about carnival, also called Mardi Gras. But you might not know about the Mardi Gras Indians. They were (and still are) one of the famous Mardi Gras "krewes," but they're lesser known and made up mostly of Black revelers from New Orleans's inner city. The Indians are organized into more than thirty "tribes," and they dress up for Mardi Gras in colorful clothes based on Native American ceremonial dress. Often, it was the Mardi Gras Indians who would organize and walk in our Super Sunday second lines.

The second line has been called "a jazz funeral without a body." It's a long street celebration with two groups of people, or "lines." The first line includes a grand marshal and a brass band: trombone, trumpet, and clarinet players, all playing jazz or New Orleans R&B. The second line is made up of the people celebrating. If you see a second line, you'll see hundreds of folks walking in fancy outfits, strutting and dancing to the music, carrying parasols, and waving handkerchiefs at the people watching. There's nothing else like it.

Our church was uptown, in New Orleans Central City, in the heart of where Super Sunday happens. During Mardi Gras, when we went to leave Sunday service, we had to wait until the second line passed, because the parades filled the streets and we couldn't drive away. But I loved watching the second lines. Everybody from old folks to kids would be marching and high-stepping in their fly gear. The parades were so long that sometimes we'd have to wait for half an hour before we could leave. We didn't care. Second lines were (and are) a huge part of what makes New Orleans New Orleans.

Second lines have always been full of colorful characters. New Orleans has always been a city of street characters, maybe because we're not really one thing. The city is a mix of Cajun, Cuban, African, French—like its own gumbo. People come to New Orleans because they can be whoever they want to be. I remember hearing about Ruthie the Duck Girl, who was famous for wandering the French Quarter with a little flock of ducks following her, while locals would buy her drinks. Another character I heard about was known as "Chicken Man," who portrayed himself as a voodoo practitioner and would shock tourists by eating fire, sticking needles into his throat, and even biting the heads off live chickens.

These days, we've got Terrylyn Dorsey, otherwise known as Second Line Shorty. She's become a main character in second lines because she dances with such enthusiasm. People go to the parades just to watch Second Line Shorty do her thing. I've had her in some of my videos. There's also a young man named Ja'Ron Cosey, who's been killing it in second lines recently. He's the son of the late Jerome Cosey, a beloved local bounce rapper also known as 5th Ward Weebie, an artist I loved and collaborated with on my record *Bounce & Soul*. There's also a guy who goes by Itchy on

Instagram who makes amazing videos of second lines and captures all the up-and-coming characters. You're nobody on the second line scene until Itchy films you.

Anyway, those second lines were so normal that I didn't even realize they were something special until I got older and moved away.

One of my other favorite early New Orleans memories is of going to the French Quarter on weekends. We'd go to Jackson Square, where all the tourists go, and hang out hoping to see the street performers who would do acrobatics for tips. We'd sit on the steps by Café Du Monde—I wasn't driving yet so I couldn't go to that many places, mainly the mall or the Quarter—and watch them do crazy backflips or stand on each other's shoulders. Then I'd go into Café Du Monde and get a warm beignet and a chocolate milk.

That was growing up in New Orleans, in a nutshell. For me, as a young boy, it was a place of family warmth, music, good friends, and unforgettable characters. It's just home.

Chapter Two

Practicing

If my family and the place we call home were the first important influences on my life, the second was music.

My parents discouraged us from listening to secular music, and it was not allowed at all on Sundays, but gospel music was a part of our lives from as early as I can remember. In addition to being a man of God, my father was also a professional musician and recording artist with a fantastic voice. When he took over Greater St. Stephen, he quickly made it one of the most musical churches in the country, but because of his high professional standards for music, he couldn't have just any musicians in his church. *Oh no.* He'd grown up near Detroit, which had Motown and was also the center of gospel, with big names like Fred Hammond and the Clark Sisters. My dad had to have the best musicians and the best production values he could find, so he exported Detroit-style recording and producing to New Orleans.

Before too long, he was recording albums with the church choir and working with incredible songwriters like Elvin Ross,

A.J. Littleton, and Michael Robinson. From the time I was about six years old, I watched professional musicians set up in our church, run sound checks, and tune their instruments. It was fascinating. It was my first time seeing how an album was created, and I gained a lot of insight into how great music came to be.

But that sort of thing wasn't common in New Orleans. It's always been a live music town, where you might go to a club on Frenchmen Street on a Saturday night and find a hot jazz combo, but there wasn't much of a recording scene. But my dad wanted to record, and he did, which brought a whole new kind of energy to the church, and a whole new dimension to my life.

My mom isn't a musician (though she can sing and loves music), but she played her own role in my becoming one. She's a great storyteller. When I was young, she could make anything sound interesting, and she's still got that gift, which is why we can talk for hours. When my younger sister, Christiann, was a baby, Mom bought a CD of popular songs that had been turned into lullabies. One of the songs was "Hey Jude," and when I told her I didn't know who the Beatles were, she told me all about them— where they came from, how they had these cool haircuts, and how the cute one who was always smiling was named Paul, like me.

I remember thinking, *My name is Paul, so I could probably make songs like that.* She told me she thought I could, too. Mom always made me feel that my dreams were possible. It didn't matter what I was imagining; she told me I could do it.

One of the reasons she and I were close was because she thought outside the box. As the only son of a preacher, I knew there were expectations on me—that people in the church assumed I would stay inside a certain box—so I needed that from her. She was the one I would tell my ideas to, and she was the one I played my new songs for first. Even though my dad called me a genius all my life, she was my encourager.

~

When I was seven, the gospel group Commissioned came to our church with their big stage production and huge amplifiers, and that showed me what was possible with a live show. I had never heard music that loud before; it was like a rock concert. After the show, I waited nervously for the members of the group by the stairs, my pad and pen in my hand, so I could get their autographs. It was like a whole new world was opening up before me.

But my close-up personal introduction to music came during those Morton family Christmases I told you about. Practically everybody in my dad's family was musical, so when we all got together for the holidays, he insisted that we hold a Morton family talent competition. If you happened to be walking by our house on one of those brisk late December evenings, you would see lights in every window and hear people singing gospel songs or Christmas carols, with others playing piano, guitar, or drums, and dozens more laughing, clapping, and cheering.

Who wouldn't want to have a Christmas like that every year? Here were instruments I could touch and people who knew how to play them and would show me how. I tried playing the drums when I was just three, then the guitar (I can play a little bit of bass, too). But when I was eight and sat down at the piano, that was it. The sound moved me, and soon it was clear that the keyboard would be my instrument.

Around 1983, Dad started videotaping all our Christmas fun, which is why somewhere there is a video clip of me at nine or ten years old playing some bluesy gospel chords during one of our Christmas celebrations. I sat at the piano with a look of deep concentration on my face while my aunts milled around in the background wearing festive red or green blouses, carrying drinks and plates of food, and shouting encouragement. When I rewatch those videos, I can see myself getting better and better on the piano every year—going from just making sounds, to playing chords, to playing progressions, to making up songs.

Around that same time, I also got to see how music was written and produced. I went to a mixing session at Ultrasonic Studios, a historic recording studio in the Uptown district near Xavier University. Some of New Orleans's greatest musicians had recorded at Ultrasonic, including Dr. John, Clarence "Gatemouth" Brown, and Fats Domino. (Sadly, it would be destroyed in Hurricane Katrina.) When I walked in, it was like Disneyland: professional producers and engineers in soundproof studios, pushing sliders up and down on huge mixing boards while recording and overdubbing tracks and laying down beats. Meanwhile, songwriters were seated at electric keyboards writing lyrics and composing melodies on the spot.

I imagined that one day, I might do what those people were doing: work in a studio and create my own original music. I had a front row seat to see how records were made, and from that point on, I ate, drank, and slept music.

I started playing piano at home, learning the songs that I heard from TV shows like *The Golden Girls*, *All in the Family*, and *Family Ties*. I taught myself to play that way, by ear, sitting in the living room and listening to those theme songs over and over. I also started trying to learn everything I could from the professionals who played in our church. During Sunday services, I sometimes sat on the stage near the drummer so I could listen to how he kept time, the different beats he played, and how the different drums sounded: the sharp snap of the snare, the echo of the toms, and the dull thud of the bass drum.

For me, the biggest influence from our church was Joey Britton, the organist who married my cousin Natalie. He had been a child prodigy in Detroit, so good on the organ that he would play as a child even though his legs were too short to reach the pedals. When Joey was eighteen or nineteen, my father moved him from Detroit to New Orleans and I got to watch him play all the time. He's a songwriter, producer, and arranger and an important figure at Greater St. Stephen and in the New Orleans gospel community.

Joey's playing blew my mind. He was a virtuoso, and like me, he couldn't read music. He played by ear. To me, he was the coolest person on the planet, from the way he dressed—so cool in a suit with no tie, like a jazz musician—to the way he played. I became obsessed with doing everything just like Joey. When I became good enough on the piano, I would join the weekly church band rehearsals and sit next to him at the piano while he played the organ. If I made a mistake, he would snap, "Stop playing," and the rehearsal would come to a halt. Then, "Start again."

Joey was tough on me, but I started to pick up finer points like chord fingerings and dynamics. I was learning how to make music. Sometimes during Sunday service, while my father was standing in the pulpit making the rafters shake with his sermon, I sat at the organ silently running my fingers over the keyboard (slowly, so no one in the congregation would notice), hearing different chord progressions in my mind, and mentally composing melodies instead of paying attention to the Word.

My dad was so excited by my developing musical interests that even when he found out about my Sunday morning songwriting sessions, he was more tickled than angry. By the time I was twelve, I had become a solid pianist and keyboard player and started to think that music might be something I wanted to do with my life. I had joined the church youth band, so I was getting to play regularly. I loved everything to do with music and being a musician.

~

When I was twelve, I did something else that most aspiring professional musicians do eventually: I started a band. (Some of the guys from that band still play with me on tour; we were born into friendship.) Every year, my dad puts on a banquet and hands out college scholarships, and in 1993 they needed live music. My godfather, a legendary fight promoter named Don Hubbard, who brought the title rematch between Muhammad Ali and Leon Spinks to New Orleans in 1978, got our band to do it.

I started the band with guys from church. One of my oldest friends, Big Ed Clark, was on drums, with my other buddies Jevon, Gary, Tim, and Sheldon (my oldest friend) on other instruments. We were called Christians Combined, which is a terrible name, but at the time I liked the alliteration. I wasn't singing or writing yet, so we were purely instrumental. We played the banquet in matching vests of all different colors and thought we were killing it.

That experience led me to start another group when I was fourteen, making it a pivotal time for my development as a musician. It was a gospel choir called God's Property (not to be confused with Kirk Franklin's popular choir, God's Property), which

I started with my friend Gino Iglehart. Gospel choirs were cool at the time, and by starting one, I was staying in the safe confines of the gospel world, which made my parents happy. I wrote my first song with God's Property: our theme song, also titled "God's Property." It wasn't a very good song, but it was my first attempt at being a songwriter, and I felt comfortable enough singing it in front of people at church.

I also honed my skills playing with Big Ed as the backing band for area vocal groups. I'll get back to that in a minute, but let me take this chance to talk about Big Ed Clark. He's from New Orleans like me, and I've known him since I was eight years old. I know we met at church, but I don't remember exactly how. I feel like Ed's always just been in my life.

When we formed Christians Combined, Ed's dad (a deacon at our church) became our manager. We would rehearse at Ed's house, which was also the party house in elementary school and junior high. Ed would dance at parties, which was fun because while he's a big dude, he's a great dancer. It was fun to hang with him at his house, or pretty much anywhere else.

So Ed and I grew up together as musicians, playing in church and listening to the real professionals do their thing, hoping to pick up some tricks. Even though he's a drummer, Ed has perfect pitch. When my dad would start doing what Black churches call "whooping," preaching with a rhythmic, musical energy until he was more singing than talking, Ed would lean over and whisper, "E flat," "G natural," or whatever pitch my dad was on. I don't know how he did it.

Ed's two years older than me, so when I got to high school, he was already there, and he became my protector. He's a big, sweet, soft-spoken teddy bear of a guy whom everybody loves, but back then his size made him intimidating. So from the jump, I had a built-in protector, this big football player who's my boy. I never needed his protection, but it was still nice to know he was there.

Ed left to go to college at Grambling while I was still in high school, and I left for Morehouse before he got back. Those were the only years we've ever been apart. During college, when I went to start my band Freestyle Nation, I couldn't find a drummer. Everybody was just a gun for hire playing multiple gigs. So I said, *Let me see what Ed is doing.* Turns out he had moved back to New Orleans and was just playing in the French Quarter and at church. That's respectable work, but I knew he was too talented to be a local drummer that nobody outside New Orleans ever saw play. Plus, nobody gets my sound the way Big Ed gets my sound.

So I went back and got him. Today, he's become synonymous with my sound, and I've always loved the way he plays drums, no matter what kind of kit he has in front of him. When we played live in the early days, we didn't have the luxury of having the best gear, but he could make trash sound so good!

But my favorite thing about Ed is that for the last fifteen years, we've checked in with each other every Friday like clockwork. He'll call and say, "Yo, you listen to the new Usher album?" or whatever, and then we'll spend hours breaking it down. Also, Ed will go anywhere for me. He's my ride or die. After college, I wanted to do some playing on the road and I said, "Hey, Ed, let's go to London." I couldn't afford to pay him, but he's just so chill that he shrugged and said, "Okay, whatever." That's always his answer. When I said, "Come on, man, we're going to Africa," in 2023, he replied, "Oh, dope." I don't ever doubt Big Ed.

Around the time I turned fifteen, Ed and I landed a dream gig: playing the House of Blues. These three artists—Jabal, Melanie, and Erica—had formed a group called New Beginnings, and they were set to perform at the famous Sunday morning gospel brunch. But they needed a backing band. They knew me and Ed from church and asked us if we could put something together, so we became the house band for those Sunday performances, with Ed on drums and me playing a two-level keyboard where I could play bass on top. We brought church to gospel brunch!

I'd never been able to get into the House of Blues because I was too young. Now I was playing there. It was crazy. The breakfast was good, and they let us eat. But I had to miss church, which was a big deal. *I'm working; I can't be at church because I've got a gig.* We played there only three times, but it was the first time I felt like a professional musician.

One other thing I remember about the House of Blues is the way it smelled. Only the House of Blues in New Orleans smells that way—like oil and candles. I don't know if it has to do with the wood, and I've never seen any incense burning, but as soon as I smell that, I'm back in New Orleans playing the gospel brunch.

At those shows, there was a guy who called himself Jo "Cool" Davis, a colorful, old school character straight out of a movie. He would always say to me, "I know your mama. I grew up in Central City. I know your mama." He was light-skinned with a bald head and a gold tooth, and would wear brightly colored suits. He was a quasi–master of ceremonies, and then after him came the host, a singer named Lyle Henderson. Joe "Cool" Davis would introduce him by saying, "Now I'm bringing on the little man with the big voice."

Lyle came on, performed a few songs, and Ed and I accompanied him while the people in their Sunday suits and dresses smiled and clapped. Finally, everybody got up and went to the brunch buffet for their waffles and bananas Foster, and New Beginnings came on.

Between the host and the trio, we usually played for at least three hours, all the while smelling eggs and maple syrup and getting hungrier and hungrier. We played and the people ate, and the trio did a second-half program of gospel songs. "When the Saints Go Marching In" was always the finale. We earned our money; I was soaked with sweat and exhausted when we finished. But man, those were good times.

The other thing I remember about the House of Blues is the Sold Out Show Wall, where the management would put the name of any act that had sold out the place. Every time, I checked out that wall to learn who had played there and how many times they had filled every seat. You can still see the wall today. Next to the artist's name, there's a hashmark for each time they've sold the place out. The Neville Brothers, Johnny Winter, Tito Puente...it's quite a list. I promised myself that I would be up there one day.

You know what? My name's up there! I've sold out the House of Blues. Pretty cool, huh? Ed and I are still playing together, too. We've gotten better musically, but our connection and our non-verbal communication are still the same. He's my rock. If I make a change mid-show, all I have to do is look at him and I know he's thinking, *I've got you.*

Up until this time, I'd only ever played gospel. My dad was a gospel artist. That music was all around me, and everyone assumed that I would eventually become a gospel musician. But then one day my friend Gino, from God's Property, gave me a cassette that would change my life. It was a tape of Stevie Wonder songs. I don't remember if it was an original album, a mixtape, or *Greatest Hits,*

Vol. 2, but I know that it had the track "I Never Dreamed You'd Leave in Summer" on it, and that it was like nothing I had ever heard before.

Hearing Stevie Wonder's music didn't just change my life. It changed my musical brain. It changed *me.* From that moment on, even though I didn't know it at the time, my future was decided.

⁓

Stevie is one of the great musical geniuses of all time. He's influenced multiple generations of musicians, but with me, the influence goes a few layers deeper. Because I was born in 1981, I had heard his later music and songs like "I Just Called to Say I Love You" and "Part-Time Lover," but I wasn't familiar with incredible records like *Songs in the Key of Life* or *Innervisions.*

That summer, when I was fourteen, I began to explore Stevie's full catalog, and that was the beginning of my real education in what it meant to be a musical artist. The music I heard on Gino's cassette blew my mind. I had never heard anything like Stevie's melodies, arrangements, or lyrics before. I had never even *imagined* anything like them.

Consider the song "Happier than the Morning Sun," off *Music of My Mind.* It's almost like a folk song. The song "Summer Soft" is as soft as summer and so creative, treating the seasons as a woman and a man and climbing higher and higher with the key changes at the end. I had never heard music like this before. I became obsessed. Gino also gave me the live record by Donny Hathaway, which had a powerful impact on what my own live shows would eventually sound like. Learning about those two artists changed everything for me.

I became a fanatic. Every week I would take my allowance, run to the Circuit City store near my house, and buy a new Stevie album, starting with the earliest record I could find. (I think *Music of My Mind* was first.) Then, week by week, I collected and consumed everything else in his catalog. Week by week, I was blown away all over again.

Stevie was so prolific. *Music of My Mind* was his fourteenth studio album, and he released it in 1972 when he was just twenty-two years old! Between 1968 and 1976 he released *For Once in My Life; My Cherie Amour; Signed, Sealed & Delivered; Music of My Mind; Innervisions;* and *Songs in the Key of Life*—six of the greatest albums in the history of popular music. Those six records alone would have been a brilliant career for some artists, but it was just one phase for Stevie Wonder. Unbelievable.

I listened to those records nonstop and I made Ed listen to them, too, until he was sick of them. For about two years, I listened to them over and over again. I took in how Stevie constructed his songs, how he built his grooves, and what he said in his lyrics. I don't think it's exaggerating to say that I exist today as an artist because of Stevie Wonder.

What I admire more than anything about Stevie isn't who he was, but who he is. He's seventy-four and still loves playing. You would think he'd be tired of playing "My Cherie Amour" after all these years, but he'll sit down at the piano and just play it without you asking. I've watched him do it. He still loves it. He's the one who made me think, *I can still stay in love with this, but I've got to keep people out who make it hard to keep that love.*

~

At the same time, I was also falling in love with other kinds of popular music. I was also starting to think like a songwriter, and my biggest influences, apart from Stevie, were the Beatles and James Taylor.

I had already come into contact with the Beatles' music when my mom introduced me to "Hey Jude" as a lullaby for my sister, Christiann, but now I dug deeper. Paul McCartney's melodies in particular caught my attention. "Yesterday" is such a simple, perfect song that says all it has to say. It's so sincere. "Strawberry Fields Forever," which was actually written by John Lennon, takes you to another world with its melody. They're two of my favorites.

I also loved the subjects that Paul, John, and George Harrison wrote about. Early on, the Beatles wrote and recorded mostly love songs, but later they expanded into topics ranging from memories ("In My Life"), social commentary about life in Great Britain ("Taxman"), and even the American civil rights movement ("Blackbird"). That was the kind of songwriter I wanted to be. Like I did with Stevie, I went through their albums chronologically, so I could experience their music as it was when it first came out and follow their development as songwriters and musicians.

When I started to investigate other kinds of music, I found the Beatles' influence everywhere I looked. Like Stevie, they became an obsession. Then, when I was sixteen, I learned about James Taylor. I was watching a TV awards show and he was getting a lifetime achievement award, but when he walked to the podium to accept, the venue played "Fire and Rain" over the PA system. My eyes flew open and I thought, *What is that song?* Remember, we didn't listen to much secular music in our house—and couldn't listen to it at all on Sundays—so I had never heard of James Taylor or the song.

I loved his voice and the fact that his songs were about such meaningful subjects (including "Fire and Rain," which was about his drug addiction and a friend's suicide), and I saw the connection. Apple Records, the Beatles' label, had signed James Taylor as its first artist. I was discovering music that wasn't new but meant everything to me.

My friends weren't into the Beatles and James Taylor. They were interested in rap and hip-hop. When I dug into those genres, I found artists like Missy Elliott, Timbaland, and Busta Rhymes, whose music was both intensely rhythmic and melodic. Busta in particular used a lot of syncopated beats, like in jazz, which I found very cool.

There was no escape for my poor family members. Once, Jasmine and I were driving to Atlanta and I put on a James Taylor CD. I made her listen to songs like "Sweet Baby James" and "Carolina in My Mind," over and over again on the seven-hour drive.

Those influences changed me. I wanted to make melodies as intricate and beautiful as my idols'. It's no accident that I won my first Grammy for my cover of the Bee Gees' "How Deep Is Your Love," which came from the same era that birthed the singer-songwriter movement, which introduced the world to artists like Bob Dylan and Joni Mitchell, who wrote and performed their own songs on piano or acoustic guitar. I can see the strands between those years of discovery and the rest of my career. Those melodies spoke to me. They were as soulful as anything in gospel.

Gradually, I was leaving behind the gospel music world and discovering a new world that had nothing to do with the culture in which I'd been raised.

~

Practicing

After the House of Blues, I was hungry for more professional gigs, but I was too young to play at places that served alcohol. That meant my other gigs were at churches—playing for gospel groups and playing midnight musicals at the city's big churches. Those were dope, like rock concerts, starting late and going for hours, with different choirs and ensembles singing and praising.

While the musicals weren't competitions, they sort of *were* competitions, if you know what I mean. Everybody was trying to outdo each other. These were the best musicians in the world to me, these gospel guys; they could really play. Playing live like that helped me hone my ear and my skills and prepared me for everything that came after.

I became one of the in-demand piano players in the city. My dad was cool about it, because he understood that I was a good kid and I was doing what I loved, so I didn't have a curfew. However, when I came home one time at about three o'clock one morning, he put his foot down. He was okay with giving me the freedom to play, but he wasn't going to let me abuse the privilege. I didn't break the rules after that.

All my live performing also taught me how to build a show. I enjoyed coming up with songs and putting together sets. I already knew I could play pretty well, but I wanted to start expressing myself. That pushed me more fully into songwriting, and I began to explore my voice as a composer and lyricist. But there was one thing I wasn't interested in doing: *being the frontman.*

For years, in every band I was in, I tried not to be the lead singer. If I did sing, it was because there was nobody else. Back then I had no interest in being an independent artist writing, singing, and producing my own songs. All I wanted to do was be one of the musicians in the background. I wanted to play keyboard, make music for people, and not be noticed. I wanted to have a band like the Beatles where I could write, play, sing harmony, and be anonymous.

In fact, I was so comfortable as a background performer that the only reason I wound up producing and singing was because I got frustrated with artists or producers who couldn't do what I had in mind. I would be working in the studio with someone, and after watching them struggle to paint with the vocal feel I wanted, or to make a track sound like what I heard in my head, I would say, "You know what? Never mind, I've got this," and take over.

I wasn't trying to be disrespectful; I just knew what I wanted. I tried to be collaborative, but I knew I was at my best when I worked alone because I could do my own thing. Still, I wanted to make everybody happy (I'm a bit of a people pleaser), so I learned to produce tracks, write, and sing in collaboration with other people. But I was still a reluctant singer. I wasn't even sure if I liked my voice. What was becoming clear, though, was that no one else was going to be passionate about my musical ambitions but me. I would have to find my own way.

Meanwhile, everything at home was about the church and gospel music. Still, for a preacher's kid, my boundaries were pretty loose. Even though my dad didn't want us listening to secular music, we couldn't help hearing the pop music of the day. We would hear Michael Jackson and Prince on the car radio and at parties, because how could we not? But the unwritten rule was that I wasn't supposed to be listening to vulgar music.

Like all teenagers, I rebelled against my parents' rules. In my case, I listened to hip-hop. Once, I had headphones on at home and was listening to MC Hammer, whose music was relatively clean, and I sang along with a lyric, "Turn this mother—" I didn't even say the second half of the word, but my mom still glared at me.

When I was older and driving, my father was moving my car and there was a Missy Elliott CD in the player. When he started the engine, on came Busta Rhymes saying, "Yo, Missy, f**k that!" My dad marched up to me with the CD in his hand and said, "Boy, what do you listen to?" Then he broke it in half and threw it in the trash. (I bought another copy.)

~

With all this going on, I was coming to a critical time in my life. I had started high school and was thinking about college, but more than that, I was starting to think like an independent musician without even knowing what that was, or how the music industry worked. It's not surprising that my two greatest influences— Stevie and the Beatles—were pioneers who set musical trends instead of following them. Both were ahead of their time, which meant the music industry couldn't control them.

But even as my interests started to venture beyond the boundaries of gospel music, I started to feel isolated and lonely. There was an unspoken expectation throughout our church community that I would succeed my father as pastor, and since it looked like I had inherited his passion for music, that I would also be a gospel musician. But my tastes and ambitions were changing in unexpected ways no one else in New Orleans seemed to understand.

I knew my father assumed I would become a gospel musician, and while he didn't pressure me, I knew that's what he hoped for. But was that what I wanted? I wasn't sure, not yet. During hours of listening to Stevie Wonder, the Beatles, and so many other secular musicians—absorbing the music, lyrics, production values, and artistic vision—I started to envision a future that deviated from the path my family and the people at our church intended for me to walk. I knew it was possible to make a living as a professional musician outside the world of gospel. People did that. They built thriving careers while making music that was moving and even spiritual, without being centered on the Word and the Lord.

I didn't know a thing about record labels, radio airplay, touring, or stuff like that. My dad and I talked about what kind of career I might have in music, but in his mind I was still *his* musician. He knew I could write, and I even placed a song on his church album. But that was through a family connection. I had no idea how you got songs in the hands of the big producers and artists in the secular world. But I already knew that if I made a career in music, I wanted to make the kind of music *I* wanted to make, not music that my family wanted me to make or that some record executive told me I had to make.

I didn't know what my authentic voice was yet, but I knew I *had* to make it heard.

Chapter Three

Religion

The third powerful influence on my life was, of course, the church.

The church was present in every part of our lives, even on vacation. We would go to places like Pompano Beach, Florida, or Myrtle Beach, South Carolina, and even there, we would go to church on Sundays. One year, we went to the Bahamas, and sure enough, this pastor came to see my dad and we went to Mount Tabor, this nondenominational church in Nassau. That was just our life.

Church translated everywhere. My dad would plan road trips just so we could go and see pastors he admired in the pulpit, like he was a sports fan going to see his favorite player. He loved church. He would have religious channels on all the time at home, watching other preachers to see what he could learn. In a way, he was like me watching music documentaries and trying to find something I can bring into my music or my live shows.

He'd watch church services, or he'd watch *The Andy Griffith Show*. Mayberry or church, my dad loved them both.

Like his father, my dad is known in Christendom as a big-time innovator. He grew up COGIC (Church of God in Christ), but Greater St. Stephen (or, as we call it, GSS) was a Baptist church, so when he became pastor in 1974, it was like a mixed marriage. People in the Pentecostal world didn't think Baptists were really saved. So my dad set about bringing the spiritual tradition of his church—speaking in tongues, healing, and all of that—into the Baptist church.

He started with just six hundred and forty-seven members, but like my grandfather, he was on the cutting edge. Eventually, we had one church in uptown New Orleans, another in New Orleans East, another across the river on the West Bank, and twenty thousand members. My dad was trying to meet people where they lived. If someone lived across the Mississippi River and wanted to attend St. Stephen, but didn't want to drive to New Orleans East, he gave them somewhere to go. At its peak, the church offered eight worship services per week, with five services on Sundays.

Sunday service was the best part of church. To me, Sunday was akin to a show about to happen. I would hear kids complain about their grandmothers dragging them to church, but that wasn't my experience at all. Church was fun. I wanted to go. I was there four or five times every week, including deliverance service on Tuesdays, Bible study on Wednesdays, and choir rehearsal on Thursdays. That's where I would see all my friends. Church was where we met up and hung out. That's where the music was. That's where we grew up together.

My dad was in charge on Sundays, and if there's one thing you need to know about him, it's that the man is *punctual*. There was a traditional 8:00 a.m. service that most of the older folks would come to, and a 10:00 a.m. service that the younger people and college students would come to, and believe me when I tell you that both services started on time and not a second later. If you were five minutes late, you missed something.

Starting on time was more important than you might think. One of the reasons my dad became a leader to a lot of other pastors is because he found a way to be innovative and congregation-friendly and still give everyone the experience of church. Before he came along, people used to think you moved with the spirit...no matter how long it took. Services could easily go for three or three-and-a-half hours...or more. They were exhausting. No matter how much they might love the Lord, some folks didn't want to give up their entire morning to go to church. My dad changed that, especially in Black churches. He said, "God is a God of order. We're not defying God by having order and saying that we're going to come at this time and be out by this time."

By the time I was twelve, our New Orleans East congregation celebrated Sundays in a brand-new, state-of-the-art building. This was not an old brick church from the nineteenth century. This was a *destination* with a professional-quality audio system. It still looked like a church on the inside, with pews and a soaring cathedral ceiling, but when you walked in and saw the giant speakers, the choir stand, and the big stage, you knew this was a venue, a place built for amplification. Our church was made for events and live performances. My dad wanted somebody to be able to stand on the stage, even without a microphone, and speak or play and know that everyone would hear it.

The New Orleans East church fit twelve hundred people comfortably, and could hold two thousand. On Sundays, it would be *packed*. If you wanted to get a good seat, you got there early. Folks would show up full of energy, talking to each other and hugging friends they hadn't seen all week. They wanted to be there. This was a place to see and be seen, the heart of the community. Sunday mornings were exciting.

Everybody came to church in nice suits and dresses, but we were less formal than some other churches where you might see women in big, fancy hats and men in expensive suits in colors like olive, violet, or camel. If it was Come As You Are month, you could wear whatever you wanted. But if it was a special day, like a church anniversary or Women's Day, we might get fancy. Everybody would wear the same colors on Women's Day, and on Men's Day, we would have an all-male choir. On Youth Day, we youngsters would take over. There was always something to look forward to. The congregation was *engaged*.

Finally, exactly at 7:45 or 9:45, the keyboard player played an opening chord, the conversations and laughter stopped, and there was that *shushing* sound of a crowd quieting itself down. Services always started with an old-fashioned hymn like "How Great Thou Art" or "Nothing but the Blood of Jesus." This was because of the Baptist tradition, which I didn't understand at the time. We were a new church, and we didn't sing formal hymns very often; less formal, more emotional gospel songs were more our style. But I learned that we did it to connect with the foundation of who we were and where we came from.

After the hymn, there was praise and worship. The band would start with a fast song to get people on their feet, clapping their hands and singing, and then a slower worship song after that. The music was as planned as the set list at a secular concert, so everyone had to be well prepared. Because I was in the youth band, I sometimes sat with the adults, where I could watch them play and also have a front-row seat for the service. I absorbed everything I could, including how the players cued each other and changed tempos and dynamics to fit the mood.

Next came announcements. We would talk about what was happening during the week, tell people how to join the choir, and so on. We also welcomed visitors who were joining us. Because it was New Orleans, and because my dad was so well known, we almost always had visitors, including groups from France and other countries. My dad invited them to stand so the congregation could welcome them with applause.

Then the choir started singing. Our church choirs were always a spectacle. We had as many as one hundred people in the choir, and some of the best musicians in the world accompanied them, including Michael Robinson, who since passed away but who played on the big Kirk Franklin live record; Joey Britton, the brilliant keyboard player who became my mentor; and Elvin Ross, the great composer-producer-director who became Tyler Perry's right-hand man and eventually married my sister, Jasmine.

By this time the congregation was on its feet, dancing and singing to the choral music like it was a rock concert, dripping with sweat in spite of the air-conditioning and not caring.

Finally the music quieted, and it was time for my dad to bring the sermon. I watched him step to the pulpit, usually in a black, gray, or white suit, his bald head shining in the lights. Everyone sat down, and suddenly you could hear a pin drop. My dad's a dynamic, powerful speaker, and he held that congregation in the palm of his hand. I've watched him move rooms of sixty thousand people and make them all feel the same thing at the same time—even me, who's heard him speak thousands of times. I picked up on his body language, the cadence of his voice, the rhythm of his words, and how he used the silences. I use those skills today in my concerts to connect to people and meet them where they are.

He started his sermon low and slow, just talking, a mixture of spirituality and study. He was always well read and well studied on what he was talking about. But he also stayed in tune with his spirit and paid attention to be sure that what he said was connecting with the congregation.

Before long, I always saw people crying. There were also funny parts of the message where everybody was laughing. But Dad gradually wound up the energy to a fever pitch until by the end, he started "whooping," preaching and singing at the same time, like in this sermon he gave after Hurricane Katrina:

I've come to speak to somebody, 'cause I know
You don't have a minute, New Orleans, for giants to
    bother you!
Somebody tonight, a giant been working on your nerve!
But I'm here to tell you, it's over, giant! Your season is over!
I've come!
Listen to Jesus, that you might have life!
And that you might have it more abundantly!
You gotta speak it, y'all!

By this time he was preaching with his entire body, and you couldn't help but feel it! Everybody in the congregation was standing, swaying, arms uplifted, singing, applauding, shouting out the words my dad was saying, crying "Amen," and "Hallelujah!" and praising. You couldn't deny it even if you wanted to. He might go on like that for ten minutes or more until he was covered in perspiration. It was exhausting and powerful.

Eventually, my dad ended his sermon and the entire congregation was standing, worn out, cheering and praising, crying and fanning themselves. The band started playing again, and some people would feel like they wanted to change their lives. It was time for the altar call. Dad called people up and they came to him in tears. He laid hands on them, prayed with them, and ministered to them, telling them what they needed to do to be saved. I've literally seen people change their lives because of this. I've seen them come into the church one way and the next year be a different person.

Once, two famous recording artists, David Byrne of Talking Heads and Brian Eno, sampled one of my dad's sermons, and used it as part of a song called "Help Me Somebody" from their album *My Life in the Bush of Ghosts*. Isn't that crazy? It was just my dad's typical preaching on a Sunday, but I imagine either Byrne or Eno was so moved by the sermon that one of them thought, *I'm going to use some of this.* You never knew who was going to show up on Sundays. Come to think of it, Dad never did get any publishing rights or songwriting credits for that tune.

After things quieted down, we had some more announcements, and then the band played one last song to get everyone's energy up and send them out the door. That's where the younger musicians, including me, were sometimes invited to play along. If it was the last service of the day, we would stay up there and turn the song into a half-hour jam session.

We would have Jermaine Williams on bass, Big Ed on drums, and me on keys. Sometimes, Elvin would be on keys with us. We didn't always have a guitar player, but we usually had multiple keyboard players. Ronald Markham might be on keys, too. Jevon Brown, who was three or four years older than me and really advanced, would also play keys sometimes.

We would just keep playing the last song while the people were filing out of the church. Once they were gone, we'd change the song, improvise, and start vibing out until the staff told us to stop. For a long time, those were my Sunday mornings.

~

As I said, my dad has always been an innovator, and in 1994, he introduced his most important innovation yet: Full Gospel Baptist Church Fellowship, a reformation (a theological movement) that combined charismatic Christian traditions like healing with some traditional Baptist doctrine. That decision changed a generation, and it also changed the culture of the Christian church around the country. Today, music and healing on Sundays are a normal thing at Greater St. Stephen, but when I was watching him put his vision together, the changes he was proposing were innovative—and scary—to a lot of people.

The motto of this new reformation was "bridging the gap between Calvary and Pentecost." My dad's goal was to update the conservative Baptist tradition in terms of what went on at church, based on what he had experienced in COGIC. He felt there were people who needed that but who also wanted to keep the strong Baptist tradition of focusing on the blood. One of the most important changes, certainly in terms of what I was exposed to and what would impact my future, involved music on Sundays. Baptists sang hymns, but they didn't allow instruments. Electric guitars were evil because they were associated with rock and roll. In COGIC, they were all about the music. I never knew church without fantastic live music.

My dad was clear on his vision, and he didn't let anything sway him from what he knew he heard. If someone disagreed with how he was changing the church, he would say, "My vision is coming from God. This is what God is telling me to do. Whatever you're saying can't compare to what I'm hearing. So while I would love for you to be with me or support me, I've still got to do this." And his vision connected for a lot of people. It turned out that a lot of folks didn't fit into any of the boxes that COGIC or the Baptists were offering, so Dad presented something new that a lot of them could be a part of.

As I've learned in my music career, going against the grain isn't easy, and it wasn't easy for my dad, either. I watched him go through the stress of trying to recruit churches and wondering if people would reject his ideas. Sometimes he would miss Sundays to go preach to a congregation in a faraway city and talk to the pastors about his vision.

Fortunately, he found enough receptive church leaders that, in 1994, taking inspiration from Jesus's twelve disciples, he hand-picked twelve pastors from around the world who felt similarly to the way he did to help him. Most were Baptist pastors who believed in the spirit, healing, and other things that many Baptists didn't necessarily believe in, and these pastors wanted those beliefs to be reflected in their church. My dad and this handful of important pastors launched a major expansion of Full Gospel Fellowship. The fact that other leaders were willing to join him confirmed for Dad that he wasn't crazy.

More churches quickly started joining Full Gospel, and by the time the first Full Gospel Baptist Church International Conference was planned for 1995 in New Orleans, they had to hold it in the Superdome because about fifty thousand people showed up! That event turned my dad into a national leader in the faith, but it was transformational for me, too.

I was fourteen that first year (an important age for me), and I made hundreds of new friends and met young people from all over the country. I met guys from Texas and from Detroit who are my friends to this day, and it turned out we had similar ideas about music and life beyond the church. Most other kids were around my age, and even though most of them weren't musicians, I met some guys who were just as good as I was, and a few who were better. I started feeling less alone. We were all PKs— preachers' kids.

My dad started holding the conferences every year, and I couldn't wait for them because friends I never saw were coming to town. I felt out of place in New Orleans a lot of the time. My thoughts and dreams seemed too big, so I would keep them to myself because I knew most people wouldn't understand. Now I was finding people who thought like I thought, people I couldn't find in New Orleans. Even better, while the main conference would be in the main facility, the youth conference was off on its own in a separate building, which meant we got to do our own thing without interference from the adults.

I made friends like Ay'Ron Lewis, a keyboard player like me. He was one of the first guys where I found myself thinking, *Whoa, another fourteen-year-old can play like that?* He's a big gospel producer now. I met the twins, DeJaughn and DeVaughn Murphy, who were singers. There was Jovan Cohen, who was also a bishop's son and doper than other young drummers I had seen.

They were all from Michigan, and they had visions of their own, which made me feel a part of something. Their dads were bishops, too, so we understood each other. There's a certain amount of pressure in being the preacher's kid. You're in the spotlight whether you want to be or not. It's like being the president's kid. We all related to each other on that level, too.

The scene was almost like those travel sports leagues where all the kids are the cream of the crop and everybody can play. The most accomplished young Black musicians came to the conference, so if you were there, you were one of the best. At that time, I was starting to think like a gospel songwriter, but I was also into more contemporary things. A duo from Iowa called Dawkins & Dawkins had released their first record in 1993 and blew our minds by taking real beats, the stuff we liked to hear on the radio, and turning them into gospel. *That* was the music I was becoming interested in making!

After a while, we started to remix church songs. My cousin Darnell was the praise and worship leader at the conferences, and he would remix stuff by acts like the Fugees and Lauryn Hill into gospel praise and worship songs. It was dope. We'd be playing and singing the music we liked on the radio, but with gospel lyrics. Then, on one day of the conference, the youth musicians were invited to go and perform during the main service—for that first year, in the cavernous Superdome.

It was incredible, walking into that huge, dimly lit space with camera flashes going off and thousands of people cheering and praising. It was major for us, getting to play in front of the adults on the main stage. Whatever we had practiced and rehearsed during our youth services that week, including our Lauryn Hill remixes, we brought to the main stage for our ten minutes. The best young singers from all over the country were there, too, so we were like a super praise team.

I'd love to find a recording of those youth bands, because I want to hear what we sounded like. We probably weren't as good as we thought we were, but we thought we were cooler than the adults. Yeah, I'm sure we were cooler.

When we got together in the youth building, we dressed well. That was where we could be ourselves. But we still brought our best. That girl from Memphis whom I haven't seen for the whole year? She might be coming, and I wanted to look good. That's how we thought. We were kids, but we were also coming into ourselves.

But when we went to play on the main stage, we stepped it up to another level. I'm talking *GQ* style. When I was younger, there was a men's clothing store in New Orleans called Oak Tree. It wasn't super fancy, but you could get suits there that were more contemporary than what our parents were wearing to church. When we were performing, I might walk in the room wearing an olive green suit with a clean white shirt and a dope tie.

Shoes were important, too. Kenneth Cole was popular at the time. I didn't get into Gators—too Midwest for me. I wanted to be a little more subtle, a little more contemporary, a little more *GQ* than a pimp suit. Clothing was serious business for all us church kids. We were into it. Conference week was when we brought out our best looks. We knew we'd be going to three services, so we had all our outfits planned out down to the socks and the tie pins.

Full Gospel was summer camp without the bugs.

~

But even the fun and friendship of those Full Gospel conference weeks couldn't hide the fact that my musical interests were taking me somewhere my family and church didn't want me to go.

I had already written R&B songs in my private time, although I wasn't thinking *I don't want to do gospel* yet. I was writing gospel songs for other people and for myself, and I still thought gospel would be my path. I knew some cool gospel producers. Buster & Shavoni were over at Gospel Centric, where Kirk Franklin was, and they were producing some great records. I looked up to them and to pros like producer Warryn Campbell. I didn't think I had to choose between religious and secular music yet.

But by that time, I had heard Stevie Wonder. I had heard the Beatles. I was becoming more and more interested in secular music at the same time that the church I had been part of all my life was growing bigger. There's this stereotype that preachers' kids always rebel because they've been suppressed their entire lives, so they automatically do the opposite of what their parents and church want them to do. That wasn't me. I loved my dad. I loved the church. But as I became a young man, the expectation—not only that I would become a gospel musician but that I would take over my father's church—became more obvious and oppressive.

The insinuations and expectations didn't come from my dad, but from the members of our church. I started hearing them when I was just ten years old. Members of the congregation would say things like, "Oh, you're little P. The namesake. Young man, I know you're going to be just like your daddy." This was not only every Sunday, but every day. That's a lot of pressure to put on a child.

It didn't make it easier that by the time I was fourteen, Full Gospel was a massive, nationwide fellowship with tens of thousands of members. GSS was still a local New Orleans church, but my dad now had a national (even international) profile, which meant as the preacher's son, so did I. There were people in California saying to me, "Man, you're just like your dad." The pressure to be the heir came from everywhere. People would ask things like, "When you gonna start preaching? Your daddy was already preaching by the time he was your age!"

It didn't let up when I went to the Full Gospel conferences, either. In fact, it got worse. I was already the bishop's son, part of the first family of GSS, so everybody I assumed I was being groomed to take over one day. But then I became the eldest son of the first family of Full Gospel, which included thousands of churches. It was a lot.

I spent a great deal of time soul searching to make sure the way I felt wasn't just a phase. I had to be sure I wasn't "running from my calling." That's a common thing to hear in church: "You're running from your calling." I still hear it today, when I'm forty-two and have a wife and three children. People who watched me grow up will come up to me and say, "I know you got something in you. Don't you run from that! I know you're doing *that* music, but there's a bigger call for you!"

I want to say, "I've got five Grammys now. I think I found my calling!" But I don't. Those people mean well. But back when I was a kid, those same folks were desperate to put me into a box for their own comfort. If I did something that wasn't approved, if I got out of the Matrix a little bit, what did that say about them and their choices?

The church was family, and I knew they loved me, so in the end, all that pressure just made me sharpen up my understanding of what I wanted to do and why. And anyway, the members of the church weren't the ones I was afraid of disappointing. The only person whose opinion really mattered to me was my dad.

Chapter Four

My Superstar

The fourth and final important influence in my life is my relationship with my dad.

Gospel music runs deep in my family. My dad is a great solo and choral singer and an award-winning recording artist, and one of his deepest wishes was that God would make me a musician so I could carry on the family legacy. In the COGIC tradition, when he found out that I was musically inclined, he would pray over my hands while I was sleeping.

The crazy thing is, it worked! Just maybe not in the way he intended.

Only once can I remember my dad pressuring me to follow in his footsteps as a gospel musician or leader of St. Stephen and Full Gospel. Most of the time, he was the one who took the burden off me. He protected me from the expectations of my family and the people at the church who thought it was my destiny. I knew he wanted me to follow in his footsteps, but he never said a word about it. Instead, he loosened that pressure valve.

I was a year or two out of college, living in Atlanta, and I was thinking about moving to New York so I could continue growing as a songwriter. Dad was traveling around the country preaching at other churches, just like he did when I was a kid, and I was traveling with him as his musician. One night we were driving and talking about my plans to move to New York and suddenly he said to me, "The way you realize your dream is by investing in someone else's dream."

I blinked, startled. I could feel the pain of those words as they hit me, and I just sat there silently while he kept driving. I didn't know what to say back to him. Like I said, my dad is the only person whose opinion I ever really cared about.

I don't know if he was talking about me investing in him or in our church's history, but for a minute I felt like maybe I was being selfish by turning my back on gospel music and trying to build a career as a musician instead of a preacher. He never said anything like it again, but his words did make me put off my plan to move to New York, and I stayed in Atlanta a little longer. I wanted to be a good son, and I was still helping him with the church. In the end, I guess you could say I put most of the pressure on myself.

That was the only awkward father-son moment of our travels. Otherwise, I traveled all around the country with my dad and it was great. Those trips were when we really came together. Just being with him and watching him go through his routine of finding a place to eat or preparing to preach was enlightening. I learned so much from him.

For one thing, my dad is a creature of habit. There's not a lot of room for the unexpected. That made our trips to some churches quite memorable. One time, I was sitting on the stage behind my keyboard, listening to my dad preach, when a man shouting and speaking in tongues came running up to the pulpit. Because he was a guest in someone else's church, my dad didn't react or even pause. He just kept preaching while security came and led the man away. We laughed about it after the service while we were eating dinner: "Could you believe it when that guy jumped up on the stage?" Those weird occurrences happened the whole trip, and we laughed about them every time.

~

Even though I grew up in the church, my upbringing wasn't especially strict. People think being a preacher's kid means following all sorts of Bible-based rules and regulations. For some kids, that's true, but other than not being allowed to listen to secular music, I had a lot of freedom growing up. My dad was and still is a by-the-book, do-things-the-right-way kind of guy, but when I was a kid, he was more easygoing than the teachers at the church preschool. When I got in trouble there or talked back, one of those ladies would raise an eyebrow and tell me, "You know, your daddy is right over there in his office." The clear message was *Behave yourself, or else.*

Nothing ever happened, and I think that was because my dad was aware that he'd had an incredibly strict childhood. Growing up, he and his siblings weren't allowed to watch sports or even play card games like Go Fish or Old Maid, because in the holiness church tradition, cards were the same as gambling. When he had kids of his own, he was wise enough to know that when you forbid children from doing things, it just makes them want to rebel. So he gave us a lot of space. We were expected to be polite and

49

respectful and make good decisions, but as long as we did that, we could mostly do what we wanted.

My dad is a charismatic gentleman with a huge, warm smile that lights up his whole face. He loves to laugh—if you know the trick to making him laugh. I love watching him and my mom talking and teasing each other, because my mom knows which buttons to push. She'll tease him gently, give him the right look or the right "Oh, really?" when he's saying something he thinks is very important, and he'll break into his great cackling laugh. But he can also be a deeply serious person, especially when the subject is church. When he's in the pulpit, he doesn't play. That is not a time to joke around with him.

What some people find surprising about my father is that for a man who makes his living delivering big sermons that can bring people to tears, he's shy. He doesn't talk a lot. He doesn't sing around the house, except when my mom is running late for church and he'll sit down at the piano and start playing and singing to calm his nerves. He doesn't use words frivolously, either. When he talks, he wants to say something. It never bothered me that sometimes when I was growing up, the five of us might all be in the house but not really talking to each other. We didn't need to. We were a warm, tight family, and we knew we loved each other. We didn't need to check in for reassurance.

I never knew anything different, but when she first met my family, my wife, Kortni, didn't get it. She talks to her mom and our son, Jakai, every day. So she would ask me, "Y'all talk or what?" And I'd be like, "We're good." That's just the Morton way.

~

When it came to music, Dad always saw more in me than I saw in myself. I started playing around on the piano at about eight years old, and from eight to twelve I was listening to songs and sitting down at the piano at church after everybody was gone, just seeing what I could do and learning about the instrument. When he found out about my love of the piano and heard me play, he started telling me, "You're a genius." He said it for my entire childhood. At first I took it as a joke, just my dad messing with me. I didn't feel any pressure because of it. But after a while, he made me believe it. I guess that's why he said it.

He was also incredibly supportive of my love of music. When I was twelve years old, I really wanted this new Casio keyboard for Christmas. Well, Bishop Paul S. Morton wasn't about to allow his only son to play just any old keyboard. When Christmas morning came and we opened our presents, I was shocked to tear the wrapping paper off a long, heavy box and find a Korg M1 synthesizer—the kind the professionals used! My dad said, "Son, you should be playing on this."

That wasn't just a one-off, either. When he found out that I wanted to start using studio equipment and recording my own tracks, Dad got Sanchez Harley, a nationally known gospel producer, to set me up with a Roland VS-1680 recording workstation with Tannoy studio speakers. I couldn't believe it. I was never ready for what he gave me. When I wanted a guitar, I thought he was going to give me a nice, simple acoustic model. Then I opened it and it was a Fender electric!

My dad supported my interest in music by always going for excellence. When he learned how serious I was about music, he said, "If you want to do this, let's go all the way." It wasn't just about getting me something expensive. Getting me top-range equipment was his way of saying, *I believe in you.* He gave me things, including his faith in my talents, that pushed me to do more and be better.

Years later, he told me that when he saw me singing around the house, he said to himself, *He wants to sing. I know he may be too shy, so I may have to just nudge him.* I knew I could sing, because I had been singing in the church choir and sang my first solo at eight on a song called "Humble Yourself." That wasn't easy. I was a shy kid, but it was expected that the son of the pastor and a great singer would be a singer, too—more of the same "He'll follow in his father's footsteps" thinking. But I was so nervous when I had to sing that I trembled all over, which was embarrassing, because that made my voice shaky and there were girls I liked in our congregation.

My dad knew exactly what he was doing. He was a patient but persistent teacher, like the light version of Joe Jackson, Michael's father, back in the days of the Jackson Five. He taught me "What a Friend We Have in Jesus" and lots of other gospel songs, but he wasn't forcing me. He was *introducing* me to the song. He would show me and then step back and let me figure it out on my own. But then when I decided to pursue music, he made sure I was one hundred percent dedicated.

He taught me every nuance of "Humble Yourself" and said, "You're my son. You're gonna get this right. We Mortons can sing. We don't play with that. So I don't care if you're a cute kid, you're gonna get this." I was almost in tears at rehearsal, but I learned the song, and managed to sing it on Sunday with all those people looking at me. However, once I started playing keys, the keyboard became my security blanket. I didn't really want to sing out in front; it made me feel too vulnerable. If I took the microphone, my hands and my legs would shake.

So when my dad came to me when I was fourteen and said, "Son, would you sing for my anniversary this year?" it took me a second to croak the words out.

"At the church? For you?"

Many churches celebrate the anniversary of their pastors coming to the community, but at GSS, our celebration was a big deal. We would have a full house, guest speakers, guest singers, and a huge party with the entire congregation. That year, 1995, marked the twenty-first anniversary of my dad taking over as pastor, and I knew my singing would mean a lot to him, so I said yes. I don't remember what I sang, but that was the year everybody saw that I *could* sing. It was also when the people of our church really started believing I was the chosen one.

But I had my own ideas. I thought I could be content sitting behind my keyboard, singing backup harmonies and staying out of the spotlight. I was also becoming more and more interested in secular music, and at the same time drifting away from my gospel roots. Eventually, when I was in college, my dad and I would have to confront this conflict between his gospel heritage and my secular aspirations.

Part Two

~

Set List

Chapter Five

Mountains and Molehills

You've seen how a lot of things started to happen for me around the time I turned fourteen. Well, there was one more. I left my mostly white middle school and started eighth grade at the prestigious St. Augustine High School, a private Catholic all-boys school that was (and still is) the leading secondary school for young Black men in Louisiana, and one of the best schools in the country for preparing young men to attend college.

St. Aug was known for academic excellence and tight discipline along with its many successful alumni, which include musician and bandleader Jon Batiste, who's won an Academy Award, a Golden Globe Award, a Grammy Award, and a BAFTA Film Award for the score for the Pixar film *Soul*; former NBA player and coach Avery Johnson; the late actor Carl Weathers, who became famous as Apollo Creed in the *Rocky* films; and Mack Maine, the rapper who would one day sign me to Young Money, my first major label. I had never been to an all-Black school, so it was an eye-opening experience.

This was the school every Black boy in New Orleans wanted to attend, and I was proud to be there. We had to wear a uniform every day—gray Dickies slacks, an oxford-style white shirt with our last name on the pocket in purple, a gray V-neck sweater, a gray tie, and black leather shoes—but we still felt cool. That combination was unique, so when you saw a bunch of Black boys in their slacks and ties, you knew they were St. Aug boys.

I loved my time in high school. There was an emphasis on discipline and making us into successful young men. The school excelled in sports and band, and was an environment that prepared us to be successful, kind of like a baby Morehouse College. In fact, when I got to Morehouse, it felt like a continuation of St. Aug. Like Morehouse, our school had its own impressive history. For example, it played the first interracial sports game in Louisiana, when the Purple Knights played basketball against the all-white Jesuit High School on February 25, 1965 (St. Aug won by twenty-two points).

Because I was with mostly the same twenty to twenty-five guys from eighth grade to graduation, we became a close-knit group. Of course, I had individual friends. Keith Taylor, who I met in second grade, was my oldest friend and went to St. Aug. He's still my friend, and a professional photographer. He shot the photos on the set of the music video for my song "Say So."

There was Sonny, who lived down the street from me. There was Peter, who lived around the corner from me. There were the Mazant twins, Paul and Germaine. Paul and I became cool because we always sat next to each other and had the same first name. We're still cool to this day. Will Williams and Brandon

Felton both ended up coming to Morehouse with me. We always looked like a crew at Morehouse because we always wore our St. Aug letterman jackets.

I have so many great memories of St. Aug, including the singer Al Jarreau being in town for JazzFest. In my sophomore year, we had a pep rally, and when we got into the gym, a band was set up there, and there was Al Jarreau. I caught Big Ed's eye across the gym and we were just like, *Can you believe this?* Probably the only people who really cared about Al Jarreau were me, Ed, and the teachers; the rest of the kids were just happy to be out of class. For me and Ed, this was our real life. We were playing the House of Blues. We were playing in church. We were professionals, just like Al Jarreau.

But the best thing I did at St. Aug was join the jazz band. By my junior year, I hadn't gotten into any activities at school. I wanted to play basketball, but in high school I stopped growing. Once I knew I wasn't going to be tall, I decided to get serious about music, and sports faded into the background.

I had seen our marching band, but I didn't even know our school had a jazz band. As soon as I found out about it, I wanted to play in it. When I walked into the room where the band practiced, it immediately felt like home. You know the typical high school band room: soundproofed walls, a central well with a piano where the director stands, the semicircular floor curving away from it in a series of risers, music stands, and other equipment scattered everywhere. Then they started playing, and that was it for me.

In a high school band, you expect to hear a few clarinets squeaking or some flat trombone notes, but there was none of that. These were the cats. They could really swing. The moment those high school boys walked into that room and took out their instruments, they went from being fifteen- and sixteen-year-olds to fifty-year-olds headlining at Preservation Hall.

These were real musicians. Their dads, grandfathers, and great-grandfathers had all been jazz players, too. Jazz was part of their legacy. Now I was dying to play with them. I had one problem: *I couldn't read music.* There was another pianist there, but while he could read, he couldn't really play. Jazz is about feel, and I had it. Plus, I knew I could play all the charts by ear. That day, I listened to the band play Duke Ellington's "Take the 'A' Train" once and I had it. I could play it like I'd been playing it all my life.

The director of the jazz band was Mr. Carl Blouin Sr., who was also the school principal as well as an accomplished trumpet player. God bless him, I know he was annoyed that I couldn't read music, but he could also see my gift, so he gave me some CDs to listen to so I could learn the songs. I took them home, sat down at our piano, and after a couple of listens I knew all the chord progressions and key changes. The next time we rehearsed, Mr. Blouin counted the group into "Take the 'A' Train"—one, two, one, two, three, four—and I was ready. When the saxophones and the trumpets started playing the famous melody, I was right there with them. Just like that, I was part of the jazz band.

~

I really grew over those five years at St. Augustine, but the most important stuff happened away from the campus. When I turned fifteen, Louisiana changed the law and I was able to get my driver's license. Then when I turned sixteen, my parents bought me my first car. It was a black Volkswagen Jetta. I had always wanted a BMW, which was beyond my parents' budget, but the new Volkswagens looked like BMWs to me. I put some rims on it, and it had tan leather seats. I still get good feelings when I think about that car.

The Jetta was supposed to arrive for my birthday, but the black one that was meant for me literally fell off the delivery truck and got all banged up. I couldn't believe it. My dad said, "Hey, they have a white one if you want it now. But if you want the black one just the way you packaged it, it's going to take a little longer." I had already told my friends at school that I was going to be driving up the next day in my new car! I knew that in an all-boys school I would take some, and they clowned on me like crazy. But I had a vision of driving exactly that car, so I was willing to wait. Eventually the car was repaired and arrived, and it was my baby.

That car became important because, right after I got my license, several people, including my brother-in-law, Elvin—who, if you remember, was a songwriter at my dad's church—told me about a recording studio on Downman Road in New Orleans East. When I got my Jetta, I started driving myself to that studio, where for seventy-five dollars an hour (which I paid out of the money I made playing gigs around the city), I could spend two or three hours recording my own songs. My father had bought me a Yamaha SY85 keyboard a few years earlier, and I had been writing songs and laying down tracks. I didn't know anything about presenting songs to artists, but I wanted to hear how my songs really sounded.

I didn't go to the studio very often—I had schoolwork and gigs, and it was expensive—but I was able to teach myself tricks I could never have learned at home, like overdubbing. At home, I had to do what we all did back in the 1990s: use cassette tapes. I'd record my vocal or instrumental tracks one at a time, each one on a different side of a cassette. Then I would play them back together from multiple cassette players and record onto *another* blank cassette. If I was lucky, I would end up with these crazy stacked harmonies. My cousin Darnell and I would do that and he would put the final recording on his voice mail greeting. Having access to a real studio changed all that.

At seventy-five dollars an hour, I could only afford to go to the studio when a song was ready to record. One of those was called "Don't Lose Your Candlestick," based on a line from Scripture about seven golden candlesticks and not losing your faith. I don't even know how I wrote it, but I let my friend Kenneth hear the studio version when it was finished, and he loved it. He told me he thought I should play it for his brother, Bryan Pierce, who had just joined the gospel group Men of Standard. They were in the middle of making their second album, *Feels Like Rain.* Bryan loved the tune, too, and when he sent it to the other members of the group, they were as enthusiastic. Just like that, they told me they wanted to put my song on the album!

It was my first placement as a songwriter. I was a sixteen-year-old high school sophomore, and I had placed a song on a major gospel record. Doesn't that happen to every teenager? I wasn't thinking about money; I was thinking about the fact that all these amazing producers and musicians were going to be making my song real. Unfortunately, everyone agreed that I was too young to produce the recording of my song, so more experienced producers—J. Moss and Paul "PDA" Allen—took over. They were masters of the craft and I soaked up everything, but something also happened during that recording session that gave me confidence that I could be a producer.

I couldn't be in the studio for the recording session, so I recorded my track for the song on my SY85 keyboard and sent

J. Moss and PDA the file. But sometimes my sequencer would get overloaded if I ran too many signals through it, and a sound would drop out, and when I was playing "Don't Lose Your Candlestick," that happened. My sequencer dropped out on the beat, and then came back in *right on the beat.* But when I sent the file and the producers sent back the full song, there was the drop in the middle of the track. J. Moss and PDA had thought my drop was intentional, and they were trying to be respectful of my song, so *they reproduced my mistake on the final record.*

I immediately knew what that meant. I thought, *They made my mistake, and they didn't know it was a mistake. I can do this myself. I'm not gonna let anyone tell me I'm not a producer.* That opened my eyes. There wasn't some secret formula to being a music producer. Technical skill and experience mattered, but so did having the sense to take advantage of accidents. I could *do* this.

After that, when I wasn't in school, I was playing gigs, working on my own arrangements on my SY85 (later, a Roland VS-1680), or at the studio when I could afford it. There, when I wasn't working on my own stuff, I would watch Elvin produce his songs. That time marked the beginning of my identity as a professional musician. I learned how recording equipment worked. I saw how experienced musicians crafted their recordings, and how the best results sometimes came from imperfection. I started thinking that I could possibly do this as a career.

But I had different music in mind from the gospel I heard every day. I wanted to be like Stevie Wonder. So while I was writing gospel in public, I had a secret life writing R&B love songs. I just hadn't let anyone know about it yet.

In the late-1990s, the New Orleans music scene was changing in exciting ways. Our hip-hop scene began to emerge. No Limit Records and Cash Money Records arrived, releasing records from New Orleans artists like Master P, Soulja Slim, Lil Wayne, B.G., and Juvenile. Bounce music, our native style of hip-hop that incorporates call-and-response and Mardi Gras Indian chants, started to gain popularity.

For me, the big news was that my song came out on the new Men of Standard record. A little while after that, I got a check for almost $3,000. My first thought was, *I'm never doing anything else.* That was it. Even more than the money I made playing at the House of Blues, that check was proof that I could have a career as a songwriter and producer. I became the most focused kid you've ever seen as far as music was concerned.

But New Orleans was so far removed from the recording industry that when I told my friends about placing a song on a Men of Standard album, they didn't believe me. That wasn't something that happened in our world. I had to bring the CD to school and show them my name on the songwriting credit to prove it.

That sums up what high school was like for me. I was kind of living a double life. By day I was a typical high school student, playing in the jazz band and hanging with my friends. I wrote our class song during my senior year. When I left campus, I turned into a real musician who had real gigs and spent time at a recording studio with professional musicians and producers. I felt like an adult in a lot of ways.

I was also learning more about myself as a professional. For one thing, I had discovered that my clear vision of what I wanted from a song made me hard to collaborate with. Call me a control freak if you want to; I'm cool with it. James Taylor made me okay with this in an interview where he said he wasn't a great collaborator, either. I had always looked at that as a negative, but James made it okay. I'm good when I do me, you do you, and then we bring it all together in the studio. But if we're trying to write together, I can't get back to my original thought. Let me have my process and control what I do.

The other thing I learned was that I had good instincts. I've always been an instinctive musician. I learned the piano by instinct. I learned to produce by instinct. I know instinctively what players I'll need for a project or a live show, and I always trust my gut. Once I believe something, if I can see how all the pieces fit together, I won't question it. I'll just do it. I'm like Nike. My instincts have never steered me wrong.

Meanwhile my parents, my family members, and the people in our church expected that I would build a career as a gospel musician, and possibly as my father's successor. There wasn't anything wrong with them believing that, because as far as they knew, I wanted the same thing. But I didn't think I did anymore. If I had given in to my people-pleasing nature and followed that path, I could've had a nice career and a nice life, but neither one would have been mine.

I still loved gospel, but in listening to Stevie and the Beatles, playing live, and writing my first songs, I knew there was no way I could stay inside that box. That wasn't the life I wanted.

~

In 1999, I graduated from St. Augustine, and like so many other kids at my school, I went away to college. I had been accepted early to Morehouse College, a Historically Black College and

University (HBCU) in Atlanta. Morehouse was the only school I applied to, in part because my mother had spun such vivid stories about her brother attending. But the real reason I wanted to go there was because I wanted to be part of the Atlanta music scene.

There didn't seem to be much else I could learn in New Orleans. I had learned how to produce, but I needed to grow as an artist, and I wanted to tour. A lot of my friends were going straight from high school to jobs in the music industry, and I didn't want to be a church musician. In New Orleans, I would always be my father's son and there would always be pressure to follow him into the gospel world.

Atlanta was becoming a force in music, like an up-and-coming Motown. The roster of artists making Atlanta their home base was impressive: Babyface, L.A. Reid, Toni Braxton, Usher, OutKast, and Jermaine Dupri, to name a few. Atlanta was on the rise and I was dying to be a part of it. I was an experienced songwriter, and Atlanta was my ticket into the R&B world. So I went to school. At worst, I would get a degree, and when I got out, I would be just twenty-one.

My dad encouraged me to leave, see other places, and have new experiences. So I left for college. For a lot of reasons, my time at Morehouse would turn out to be three and a half of the greatest years of my life.

Chapter Six

Kid Again

Morehouse College is the largest men's liberal arts college in the United States, and one of the most prestigious. Founded in 1867, it was at the heart of the 1960s civil rights movement, and throughout its history has been one of the most important centers of Black learning and success in the world. Martin Luther King Jr. went there. So did Spike Lee, Samuel L. Jackson, and civil rights leader Julian Bond. Morehouse has graduated eleven Fulbright Scholars, five Rhodes Scholars, and five Marshall Scholars, so to be a "Morehouse Man" (as its alumni are known) is quite an honor.

My mother's brother, Uncle Man, had gone to Morehouse, and it changed his life. Going there was life-changing for me, too. I was on my own for the first time, away from home, but I still had family ties. My older sister, Jasmine, went to our sister college, Spelman, which was right next door. But I wasn't in a hurry to tell everyone who I was. In New Orleans, I'd been kind of a big fish, Bishop Paul Morton's only son, a gigging musician and published songwriter.

But when I got to Morehouse, the people I met were the big fish; I was just a freshman. I could stop being a preacher's kid.

Living in New Orleans, I had dreamed every day about becoming a producer, but it was just a dream. I had always felt like a fish out of water because of my aspirations to do something big with my music. I would think, *I'm not even gonna tell people that I want to be a producer and tour and win Grammys. That sounds too crazy. Too big.* But at Morehouse, everyone was so focused and driven that the energy was contagious. The atmosphere made you want to lock into whatever your thing was.

Don't get me wrong—we had fun, too. But when it came down to it, the attitude from everybody was *I'm here because I want to be the best.* Everybody wanted to be somebody important and successful. They were all driven like I was. For the first time, my aspirations didn't make me feel out of place. I fit in *because* of them.

Then there's the "Morehouse mystique." Alumni talk about it, but when you're on campus, you can feel it. I did. I found myself thinking of the lineage of the great Black leaders who went there before me. They were people who changed the course of history. Once I had a sense of that history, I started to feel a responsibility. It wasn't pressure, exactly, but it was like I'd been handed a duty to live up to the example of the people who came before me.

It was the perfect place for me.

Everything I experienced at Morehouse was the best of the best, and was designed to prepare us to be exceptional men. When I went to freshman orientation, they told us we had to wear a suit and tie to every class. They taught us about etiquette—which fork to use at what part of a meal, which pen to use, even how to write a business plan. Some of the most incredible people in the world came to speak and share what they knew. Legendary investor Warren Buffett spoke to my business class, telling us stories about playing video games with Bill Gates, how he still lives in the same house in Omaha that he bought in 1958 for just $31,500, why he invested in Coca-Cola and Gillette, and more. Spike Lee spoke to one of my classes.

Life at Morehouse was just like that, with amazing people popping in all the time just to talk to us. Why not? We were the cream of the crop of young Black men from all over the world. When I took my son Jakai to the college in 2023 to see if he was interested in attending, the dean introduced us to a man who had fought apartheid in South Africa alongside Nelson Mandela. Later I told Jakai, "Yeah, it's like that every day. It becomes normal after a while."

~

When I walked onto the campus for the first time, it was like I was walking into the Spike Lee movie *School Daze*, but for real. I remember my parents dropped me off, then I walked up the hill to a building called the Living Learning Center, or LLC. That was my residence hall.

Being at Morehouse was a little strange at first, because a lot of these guys—including our resident advisor, Tim—were aspiring young preachers who looked up to my dad. That meant my reputation preceded me, which wasn't what I wanted, but it was okay. I lived in Room 116 with my first cousin, Jason, so I knew someone right away.

Right next to us were Marquis and Mario, twins from San Bernardino, California. Right across the hall from us was Tremaine, who was from Miami. I didn't even know that Miami had real Black people until I met Tremaine. I thought everybody from Miami was like Crockett and Tubbs from *Miami Vice*. That was my main little group of friends.

Another thing I loved about Morehouse was that it wasn't fancy or snobby. Morehouse is all about what you get from the place. No matter who your family is, everybody's on the same level. My dorm room had two little twin beds—Jason slept on the left, and I slept on the right. We brought in our own little TV and our PlayStation, and we played cards all the time.

Ours was the hot room in the LLC, the room where everybody wanted to be. We staged boxing matches, real ones where the guys used boxing gloves. Imagine twenty or thirty guys crammed into a tiny dorm room, maybe one hundred feet square, sitting on the beds and the floor, everybody sweating and cheering while two guys punched each other until someone said, "No more."

In fact, our room was almost *too* hot, because I almost flunked out. I failed accounting in my freshman year, and I almost failed another class. The problem was that we were addicted to playing spades. That was our card game, and it's still my game today. I play it all the time when I'm on tour. Jason and I were partners, and sometimes we'd finish a game and say, "All right, one more game" over and over again until we had been up all night, the sun was coming up, and we had to drop everything and rush, red-eyed, to our first class of the day.

The only time I lived on campus was freshman year, but I'll never forget it. It was so much fun just being one of the guys and learning all about college life with these young men who all were aspirational like me—who all had their own big dreams. We had people who wanted to be scientists, marketing experts, musicians, everything. I was exposed to all of that, and it changed me during that very first year.

~

But even in Atlanta, I couldn't completely escape the pull of gospel music. My cousin Jason's father, my uncle Jimmy, had a church in Atlanta, and my first job when I got to the city was playing at Uncle Jimmy's church. But when I played there, it was too familiar for my comfort. My uncle and his church couldn't have been more welcoming, and since everybody had always assumed that I was bound for a life in gospel music, it would have been easy for me to stay on that path—playing churches and building my reputation. I might as well have been back home in New Orleans, the preacher's kid again. So I quit that gig.

Next, I learned that the gentleman who had started a college gospel choir called New Life was looking for a piano player. That sounded like a perfect gig. Nobody would know me! Well, I was fooling myself. As famous as my father is, *everybody* knew who I was. But at least I had gotten the job on my own merits— not because I knew somebody or because of who my dad was, but because I could play. It was my first time landing a gig based solely on my abilities as a musician.

Still, it would have been dangerously easy for me to fall back into the gospel world. How easy? After high school, during the summer when I was moving to Atlanta, my sister Jasmine and I formed our own gospel group, Jasmine and Paul. At the same time, I was already making plans to start my own band playing R&B and soul. I wanted to create my own version of the Beatles with me as George Harrison—playing, writing and singing harmonies. In my mind, I was already moving on.

Instead, I tried Jasmine and Paul. This was my last-ditch attempt to see if I could be the gospel musician I thought my father wanted me to be. I knew I could do it musically, but I wanted to see if I could be that person. I was thinking that if I could make the music hip enough, I might be okay.

Again, I was lying to myself. What we made might not have been traditional gospel music, but like all gospel, it was always the same message. After a while I couldn't help thinking, *I want to talk about more than this*. But I tried to make everyone happy, because I knew that if Jasmine and Paul failed, I would have to confront my dad and tell him that I didn't want to follow in his footsteps. That scared me to death. So we kept going.

We even made a record, *Jasmine and Paul*. We both sang on it, but I didn't play, which was weird for me. Elvin Ross produced and let me produce three songs. But we performed live to a backing track, not a live band, because I was trying to be as contemporary as possible. That was totally alien to me, and not what I wanted my sound to be at all.

You go into a studio, put on a big set of headphones, and stand in front of a microphone covered with a "pop screen"—a round mesh screen that keeps explosive sounds like "p" and "t" from showing up on the recording—hanging from a long, telescoping boom. Then a track created by the producer starts playing, the engineer cues you, and you start singing. Depending on what the producer wants or if you're overdubbing—recording your own harmonies—you could wind up doing multiple takes until you're hoarse.

But I didn't know enough to say no. I knew about the

songwriting side of production, but I hadn't worked as a singer, so I just went with it. Elvin knew I could sing, and he knew about Jasmine's voice. We were young, attractive, talented kids, and from a marketing perspective, he knew our duo made sense. But once we released the album, I decided I couldn't continue the project and stepped away. Three years later, I would ask the producers to take the album off the iTunes store.

It wasn't that I was afraid Jasmine and Paul would fail. I was afraid we would *succeed*. This was the path of least resistance, and it was laid out for me. It would have been so easy for us to be the next big brother and sister duo, like BeBe & CeCe. My dad was so well known, and the Full Gospel network included thousands of churches all around the world. We would've had a huge built-in audience. *Oh, Bishop Morton's kids want to come here and perform? Sure.*

I knew I was turning down a sure thing. We performed at Creflo Dollar's church (where I met Jesse Bond, who became my guitarist), a huge church in Atlanta at that time. We performed at the Stellar Awards, the Grammys of gospel. I went along with some things because they made me feel like I was getting closer to my mainstream dream—doing the photo shoot for the album cover, for instance. That was exciting. But the closer we got to the album release, the more pressure I felt. I knew Jasmine and Paul could be big. I was a preacher's kid. I knew the culture, and I could fake it. But that was *not* the voice I wanted to speak with. It was eating away at me. I wanted success, but I didn't want to get it by compromising who I was.

I shut Jasmine and Paul down because I was worried that if I didn't, I'd be trapped. If I had thought it would die on its own, I might have let it play out. But I knew it wouldn't. Jay and I would become gospel stars, and once that train started rolling, there would've been no way for me to stop it.

~

By the end of my freshman year, I had no choice. I had to tell my dad that I wasn't going to become a gospel artist. He would know I had pulled the plug on Jasmine and Paul and would be wondering why. I'd done everything I could to put off the conversation, but I couldn't do it anymore. I don't think I've ever dreaded anything more than that talk.

I had tried to tell my dad how I felt two years before, when I was sixteen. My dad, my mom, my sister Christiann, and I had just finished dinner and were standing in the kitchen of our house on Wright Road, cleaning up. By this time, I had already sold a song to Men of Standard and everyone knew I was writing and producing my own love songs. My family knew something was up. But as I stood there, crying and shaking, trying to tell them that I didn't want to follow the gospel path, it felt like everybody was coming at me with questions.

"What are you doing?"

"Why are you doing this?"

"Are you trying to rebel?"

That last one brought the blood rushing to my face. Did they think this was some sort of generic teenage rebellion? The idea was insulting. That's a funny thing about being unique. Sometimes you don't have enough time to explain, so people just put you in the same box as everyone else.

Once, when I was in Africa, I got a tattoo. Some lady in the tattoo shop rolled her eyes and said, "Oh, all you Americans get a tattoo of Africa when you come here." Then I told her the story behind the tattoo, and she changed her tune. I said, "I'm not most Americans." (I'll share the story with you, too, a little bit later.) That's what I mean by the "box" mentality. If you're different, people make themselves feel more comfortable around you by putting you into a framework they can understand. That's why everyone says that preachers' kids rebel because they've been forced to conform for so long. But eventually, it's said, they come back to the fold. I was trying to tell my family that wasn't what was happening, but at sixteen years old, I didn't have the words.

But that first attempt battle-tested me. When people give you pushback, you have to make a choice. *Do I care enough? Does this mean enough to me to fight?* Trying to tell my dad showed me that when I was ready—when I cared enough—I would fight. It also made me question my motives. Was I just trying to rebel? Right away, I knew the answer was no.

I don't remember planning on calling my dad on that night two years later. It just felt like things had come to a head, so I did it. I was at Elvin's house in Atlanta, and I just called him. I hadn't told anyone that I planned to talk to him, but I had run scenario after scenario in my head, trying to figure out what to say and to predict how the call might go. But as I dialed the phone, my hand was shaking. I remember thinking, *Maybe I can just ride this out.*

I was sure what I had to say was going to shock him. When you're part of the First Family, you have to put up a facade of happiness and perfection, and I was good at it. That's why preachers' kids get that bad rap of being the worst. But we're not the worst. It's just that the expectations laid on us are sky-high, so when something happens that would be normal for another teenager, people clutch their pearls and gasp, "Not the preacher's kid!"

The line rang on the other end, and my dad picked up. "Hello?"

My mind went blank. Anything I had planned to say, I forgot. I started stammering. "Dad, I just wanted to talk to you... I don't know... I'm trying to do this, but I don't think I can..." I was shaking all over and crying.

He must have heard me trying to get it out, or trying to be careful in how I said it. But he waited until I stopped, and then he said gently, "Son, you don't have to be me."

Telling my father was the hardest thing I've ever done. I didn't want to disappoint him. He would've loved for me to be a preacher, and he already knew I wasn't doing that. Now I wasn't even going to make the music he cherished, even though he had gotten me every piece of equipment I had ever asked for. I felt like I was betraying him. Then he said those seven words and I could breathe again.

"The way you're going to change a generation is different than the way I did," he went on. I had underestimated him and his love for me. He *knew*. He had known for a long time. I don't remember what else we said on that call, but it didn't matter.

When I hung up, it felt like a ten-ton weight had fallen off my shoulders. My dad gave me permission to be who I wanted to be, and it made me not care about what anybody else said. He made me bulletproof, because his opinion was the only one I cared about. In the future, when someone questioned my choice to do secular music, I would think, *My dad is good with it. I don't really care what you think.*

I was never the same after that call. Before that conversation, I was one person. After that conversation, I was another. I was free to do me.

Chapter Seven

Sticking to My Guns

Away from the Morehouse campus, the Atlanta music scene was bubbling, and that's where I focused an increasing amount of my attention and time. I majored in marketing, but music was what I cared about most. Almost as soon as I got to Atlanta, I found a studio.

During freshman year a friend named Chuck, who I'd met at one of the Full Gospel conferences at the Louisiana Superdome, had moved to Atlanta. His brother was a songwriter, and one day Chuck took me to Noontime Studios, one of the hottest studios in the city, to meet his brother.

Noontime Studios was founded by Chris Hicks, Ryan Glover, and Henry Lee. Artists like Toni Braxton, Ginuwine, and Ludacris have recorded there. At that time, the Atlanta music scene was like nothing I had ever seen. Starting in the 1980s, the city had become an R&B mecca, led by performers like Braxton, TLC, and Bobby Brown. But by the early 2000s, Atlanta had also become a power in rap and hip-hop, just as André 3000 had predicted when he said, "The South got something to say," after OutKast won Best New Group at the 1995 Source Awards. By the early 2000s, hitmakers like Monica, Usher, Lil Jon, Ludacris, and Young Jeezy had helped Atlanta become a pop music power, stealing some of the thunder from the East Coast–West Coast rivalry.

The studio was located in Midtown Atlanta around the King Plow Arts Center. Midtown was home to Music Midtown, a big music festival created by promoters who wanted something similar to the New Orleans Jazz & Heritage Festival. When I first walked into Noontime, I saw a small office to my left, and then I walked down a hallway lined with heavy, soundproof doors, three on a side.

These were the studios. Each one had a vocal booth, a producer's desk where you could put your keyboard or drum machine, a computer with Pro Tools on it, and a digital console, which the producers used to combine and adjust the quality and levels of different audio tracks—vocals, instrumentals, beats, and so on. When I walked into Noontime on that first day, I didn't know what I could do with my songs. But all around me in those studios were guys who did, and they were turning their ideas into music.

That day showed me what was possible with the green light my dad had given me. *This is it. This is where I want to be.* That first day, I met an artist named Tank, who was there working on his album, and who's since become a successful R&B artist. I saw major producers like Teddy Bishop and Jazze Pha working the board or just walking the halls.

I walked around, my eyes wide like a kid on Christmas morning. I had never seen music made like this. I had never seen this many professionals working on records. It felt like being at Motown before it became Motown. When I stuck my head into a studio, apart from the haze of smoke, there was always something different going on. In one room, a producer was building a beat. In another, a producer was laying down a track. In another, a singer was laying down a vocal line. I was watching creativity at work in real time. Each room was assigned to a producer so they could come back and continue what they had been working on.

This was night and day from the scene in New Orleans. These were the guys who had songs on the radio and at the top of the charts. I was instantly addicted. No question, this was the world I wanted to be in. Morehouse was important, but I was going to school to get through school. This was what I wanted to do with my life.

I interacted most with two producers, Donnie Scantz and Bryan-Michael Cox. They were both from Houston and had both moved to Atlanta to work with Noontime. I mostly collaborated with Donnie, who took me under his wing and basically made me his co-writer. He was great at the drums and making beats, and he taught me how to use the MPC, a workstation for making beats. He was a drummer first, so he always had cool rhythmic ideas, but he didn't play any other instruments. So I played his keyboard parts and put melodies to his rhythmic ideas.

I didn't really collaborate with Bryan-Michael Cox, but he always had great energy and was always encouraging me. He's gone on to become one of the most successful producers of all time. Over the months, I also met Jazze Pha and songwriter Johntá Austin, who co-wrote "We Belong Together," "Don't Forget About Us," "It's Like That," and "Shake It Off" from Mariah Carey's biggest-selling album, *The Emancipation of Mimi*.

Practically overnight, I went from being totally non-industry to rolling deep with industry players. Real producers were coming up to me and asking, "You play keys? Could you play on this?" I didn't have a keyboard in my dorm room, so I would practice in Sale Hall, because there was a piano there. That's where I met the singer-songwriter Nate Wonder, who would become Janelle Monáe's producer. That's where I met Vaushaun Brooks (better known as the Grammy-winning hip-hop record producer and songwriter Maestro), who introduced me to Justin Henderson, now known as the multi-platinum songwriter and producer Henny Tha Bizness, who's produced for Drake and Lil Wayne. I'm telling you, musical talent was falling from the trees in Atlanta.

~

All this activity was still technically connected to Morehouse, but back then there wasn't a school-sanctioned path at Morehouse for students like me who wanted to pursue careers in the music business. We had to make our own path.

Noontime and the contacts I was making there were so exciting that I started living a double life. A buddy of mine, Brandon Felton, who went to St. Aug with me, had a plan to get us out of Morehouse in three years. I was down, so he said, "You've got to take no less than seventeen hours every semester, plus nine hours every summer. *Going to school year round. All right.* But I said, "Okay, let's try it."

My classes were broken up between Monday-Wednesday-Friday classes and Tuesday-Thursday classes. A typical day on Monday would be me going from 9:00 a.m. to my last class at 3:00 p.m. I would chill, change out of my Morehouse clothes and make sure my locks looked good, and then I would head for Noontime at seven or eight at night. I would go into the studio with Donnie, and we might work until after midnight.

We had a process where we traded off, back and forth. If it started with me, I might develop a chord progression on the keyboard and play it in a loop, maybe four times around. Donnie would build a beat around that idea on his MPC 3000. I'd sit back and watch him, because he was a master. Then I would come in and put a bass sound on top. That might inspire him to do something different with the drums.

We would ping-pong like that for a while, but eventually we'd have a track. At that point a songwriter might come in and write with us and we would build an entire song from there. Sometimes, that process might be broken up over several days, but if we were rolling, we might keep going until three in the morning. If we didn't have a songwriter, we might just package the track, put it on a CD, and give it to some songwriters and let them write songs to it. This is before I was really focused on songwriting; I just wanted to be a producer and make beats.

I would go back to my dorm, sleep for about four hours, then get up and go to class. It's amazing what you can do when you're eighteen or nineteen. Sometimes, I wonder how I graduated. I was in heaven, though. This was my dream come true, and the opportunity didn't exist in New Orleans. That process, that system, that thinking, that culture—they existed only in Atlanta.

~

Guys still go to Morehouse to be doctors and lawyers, but if you want to have a career in the music world, there's a path for you now at Morehouse. Henny works at Morehouse now and runs a sweet studio just for the students. He and I have stayed friends since my time there. The school even offers classes in songwriting and production. Back when I was a student, that didn't exist. Morehouse students who wanted to make a life in music had to figure it out for themselves. We had to meet people; make connections; find ways to get our songs produced, released, and heard; and hope to get signed by a major label.

The irony for me was that as happy as I was being part of professional music production, it started to feel too limiting. I didn't want to have to fit my musical voice and vision into one narrow musical genre for the sake of sales. I wanted to be my own thing. Part of those early years in Atlanta was me trying to figure out exactly what my thing was.

Every day, I was working with industry leaders producing hip-hop and R&B. On the side, I was writing my soul songs, but I couldn't see a path for me to build something with that music. Brian McKnight had put together a great career with soul, but there was no young soul singer and songwriter who had redefined the genre. D'Angelo had come out with *Brown Sugar* in 1995, and Erykah Badu had come out with *Baduizm* in 1997, and I felt more connected to that music than I did to mainstream R&B because of the strong instrumentation and arrangements. But I didn't know anyone in the neo-soul movement. I was searching for a genre and thinking that, just maybe, I would have to create one.

One of the pivotal moments in that search was meeting India.Arie. In 2000, my sophomore year, I moved off campus. In the lobby of my apartment complex there was a piano. One day I was playing and this young Black woman came over and introduced herself. We got to talking and she said, "Oh, you know, I sing a little." I asked her to sing something, and she sang Stevie Wonder's "Ribbon in the Sky." My jaw fell open. She told me she was working with Motown on her first record.

India's first record, *Acoustic Soul*, came out the following year and was nominated for seven Grammys. Unfortunately, Alicia Keys released *Songs in A Minor* the same year and she won Grammys in all the categories India was nominated in. But India and I had become friends, and when I played her a song I'd written called "Interested," she liked it and ended up recording it as a bonus track on her second record, *Voyage to India*, which I also produced. This time, she won the Grammy for Best R&B Album.

I was only twenty, but "Interested" was my first mainstream placement and my first mainstream songwriting check. More importantly, working with India opened up a part of my brain that said, *Okay, I can write about things I want to write about.* She showed me what was possible, because her record was, literally, acoustic soul. She was James Taylor. But before India, there hadn't been a place for a Black artist—and certainly not a Black woman—who combined soul with an acoustic folk feel. (No disrespect to the great Tracy Chapman.)

Around 2001, I decided it was time for me to form my own band. I still didn't want to be a solo act. I wanted to write Beatles songs, but in the soul genre. So I began pulling together musicians from around Atlanta. It was so random; I was practically picking people off the street. I grabbed one of the coldest bass players in the world, Darrell Freeman, who's still my buddy. Kim Carree, who could play keys and really sing, would be our lead singer. James Barrett was our original drummer. Finally, Charles Lamont, who plays percussion for me today, introduced me to a guitarist called Big D. That was supposed to be my first band.

We had a rehearsal, but those players just didn't have the same drive as I did. They needed to earn money and pay bills and didn't have the time for an experiment. They weren't motivated by the same things I was. Finally, around the time I was finishing at More-house (I had all the credits to graduate in 2002 but walked with my class in 2003), I let that lineup fall apart and started rounding up my friends. That's how Freestyle Nation started.

First, I accepted my fate and decided that I would be the lead singer. The next obvious move was to get Big Ed Clark to be my drummer. As always, he said, "Okay, cool." Next came a friend from Spelman, another preacher's kid named Kalilia Wilson, who went by "Sweet Lili" and could really sing. Around this time the Black Eyed Peas were getting big and I saw Lili as our Fergie.

Jesse Bond, from Reno, Nevada, was our guitar player. I'd met Jesse when my sister and I were singing as Jasmine and Paul at a church conference and his group from the Berklee College of Music in Boston came down to play. I told him, "I'm starting a band and I need a guitar player." There was one obstacle: I had never heard him play. We became friends, I moved him from Boston to Atlanta, and he lived in my house, but I still never heard him play the guitar.

That was for the best, because I had to help Jesse unlearn everything he had learned at Berklee. Berklee is one of the best music schools in the country, but they teach classical and jazz guitar following a strict form and technique. That wasn't what I needed. I needed someone who could play from the gut like me. This became a theme in my career: trusting my instincts, especially when it comes to other musicians and singers. All I need is clay I can mold, the sonic paint for the painting I want to make. If your heart is with me, I can get you to play what I want you to play.

Teaching Jesse wasn't easy. When I wrote songs on the guitar, he would look at my chord progressions and groan, "Man, that's wrong." I would say, "I don't care, this is the chord I want, so I'm playing it." It took a while to get him to look at guitar playing according to the PJ Morton rulebook. Eventually, he lightened up on the formal technique, let go of the sheet music mentality, and became the heart of the PJ Morton Sound.

What's funny about Jesse is that he's a *very* white guy, but after a while he started liking Black women. He even married a Black woman. When I met him, he was a vegetarian, but he loves barbecue now. He even started playing for the church. I think I put him through "Black bootcamp" and changed the man.

Being the only white guy in the band, he also got to experience a lot of our pain—the small racial issues and minor humiliations we had to go through every day that he didn't. For instance, sometimes we sent him to do things because we knew he'd get a different reaction from the rest of us. If we were on tour and needed to check into our hotel early, we sent Jesse to talk to the front desk. You know what I'm saying? He got to see firsthand a lot of those microaggressions that Black people have to deal with.

That sort of thing didn't happen in Atlanta, but if we were driving our fifteen-passenger bus through those little country towns in Alabama and Mississippi, Jesse was our representative. In those parts of the country, Jesse would drive a lot of the time, because if we got pulled over, he would get a different reaction from the cop. It was like living our own version of the movie *Green Book*.

Alvin "Cornbread" Garrett from Birmingham was our bass player. I gave him that nickname because I thought it sounded good and because he was an Alabama country boy. I was our keyboard player, songwriter, and lead vocalist. That was Freestyle Nation, a group of misfits. These weren't the people that everybody in Atlanta knew, but they were who I needed.

~

Right around that time, as Freestyle Nation was starting, I had one of the best moments I've ever had with my dad when he saw me play secular music live for the first time. It was 2002 and we were playing our first live gig at an Atlanta club called 7 Stages Theater.

7 Stages is still open and hosting shows in a part of Atlanta called Little Five Points, a hip, artsy, retro, Bohemian part of town. Little Five Points was where the thrift stores and the cool vinyl record stores were located; you'd go to Moreland Avenue on a Saturday to buy vintage clothing, hang out at dive bars, or get great Ethiopian and vegan food.

7 Stages was a warm, brick-lined space filled with all kinds of colorful, crazy furnishings. It felt like a café and coffeehouse as well as a performance venue. The main stage wasn't fancy, just a recess under a big concrete beam, but it was a popular spot for live music, and Freestyle Nation was there to open for this amazing R&B singer from Decatur, Georgia, named Algebra.

Our 7 Stages performance was the coming-out party for Freestyle Nation, so I invited my parents. I was nervous when I saw them in the audience, but when we came onstage and started playing—and I started singing—my dad's eyes got wider than I'd ever seen them. It was a role reversal, and I loved it. Growing up, he was always the larger-than-life figure: Bishop Paul S. Morton, singer and Full Gospel superstar. This was the first time he had seen me sing as myself, not because he asked me to in church. His expression said, *Who is this person?*

I had started to learn about my voice and how I wanted to move and talk onstage, and seeing and hearing me that way was a turning point for him. After our set, I went out into the crowd and gave him a huge hug, and he said to me, "Boy, all right, you're not shy!" I could tell he was proud. He always is when he sees me play, but that was special because it was the first time he had seen what I could really do. That was an important night for both of us.

It was also the beginning of him understanding how I was mixing the gospel and secular worlds. Later on, he said to me, "You didn't just rebel, and you're not talking about crazy sexual stuff. Okay, I can get behind this." I wasn't playing gospel, but I was performing love songs with themes that my dad could recognize and appreciate. I knew he was thinking, *He's going to be all right; he's still my son.*

~

Talking about live performance brings me to Apache Café, a restaurant, bar, and live music space on Marietta Street in Midtown Atlanta. It opened in 2001 serving jerk chicken, art, poetry, and live music. It became *the* place to go in the city to hear up-and-coming hip-hop and soul artists. The first time I ever saw Janelle Monáe was at the Apache, when she was actually opening for us. The Apache was an important gig. If you could kill it there, you could get poppin' all over Atlanta, and that was a gateway to the big time. The Apache was where Freestyle Nation honed our skills.

I played there before I ever started Freestyle Nation, first by sitting in as a keyboard player with the open mic live band, and later as a solo regular. The players who'd been there awhile told me all about a club that had been at the same address—64 Third Street, a former Laundromat—called the Yin Yang. "Oh, man, you missed the Yin Yang? It was legendary," they would say. India.Arie and Bone Crusher played there; the place was part of soul music folklore.

The Yin Yang was gone, but the Apache had the same spirit and vibe. When you went there, patrons would be outside in front and back, just chilling and drinking, sometimes hours before show-time. So the energy was high before anybody played a note. The club was small, with a capacity of two hundred to three hundred people, with tables in the front sometimes and space for standing room in the back. The stage was small, too, just big enough for a keyboard, drums, bass, and PA system. They had only one bath-room at the back of the main room.

I remember that particular detail because, one time, we were doing a show and my stomach was really upset. But there was no way I was going to go to the bathroom, because if I did, I would have to walk through the whole audience, and they would know it was me blowing up the bathroom for twenty minutes. Then I would have to come out, walk to the stage, and say, "All right, guys. I'm gonna do my show now." That was not an option. My stomach was killing me, but I had to hold it. The alternative was so much worse!

The highlight of the Apache was Wednesday open mic night. It was first come, first sing, so you had to get on the list early if you wanted to perform, and you'd better be good. The level of talent at the Apache was like nothing I've ever seen at any other open mic. You had to be brave to get up there. But if open mic Wednesdays were a big deal, the regulars were unforgettable. They showed up every week and usually performed the same songs, so the audiences knew them all and loved them. One of the regulars was a guy named Malachi, a local singer and musician. He would come in every week and sing this great song that, as far as I know, was never released by anyone. But fans knew him and his song, and they went crazy.

It was cool to see other artists find an audience of music lovers who really appreciated them. Half the audience were artists themselves, so they knew what it was like to be up there with all eyes on you. They were incredibly supportive, and the atmosphere was electric.

After I formed Freestyle Nation, I wanted to test our songs at the Apache on Wednesday nights. If we sounded great, we would have the most supportive room ever. But something told me that before we played there, we should make a record. I told the band, "When we perform, people are going to want to buy our record. So let's create it." Nobody taught me that; I knew it intuitively. So we went into the studio and after a few months we had an album, *Freeversation*. Then we played the Apache, and the crowd lit up. Our sound worked, and my songs worked.

After a while, the fans at the Apache knew when Freestyle Nation was coming, and the energy was hard to describe. Think of *Purple Rain* when they knew that Prince was about to come onstage; that was how the room felt when Freestyle Nation was getting ready to play. For young artists just trying to figure it all out, it was a priceless experience. Before too long, we started doing our own weekend shows at the Apache. Something about that room always brought out the best in us; those were some of the best shows I've ever done anywhere.

The place didn't really have a backstage. The outdoor hangout area I mentioned *was* the backstage. You want a private dressing room? Dream on. We sat outside with the crowd before the show, drinking, talking about music, and enjoying the warm nights. Before I had fans of my own, those folks were my fans. There was a lot of anticipation at the Apache because of our Wednesday appearances.

It was so casual that there wasn't even a set time when our gigs started. When the vibe felt right, we just knew it was time to start. It was like playing for a room full of your friends. We'd finish our drinks, get up, go inside, grab our instruments and mics, tune up, and start playing.

We used to end the Apache shows by playing "Where Everybody Knows Your Name," the theme song from the TV show *Cheers*. People would sing along, and that became a staple for us for years. But even before I did that, I would do this gospel song called "It Won't Be Long," by Andraé Crouch, but sung to the tune of Prince's "Purple Rain." The Apache felt like church when we did that. It was spiritual. It was like everybody was of one accord. That's what I remember most about those Apache shows. Every memory I have of the Apache—the lights, the crowd, the smell of incense—is a good memory. Everything I learned about connecting with an audience—call-and-response and all the rest—I developed there.

Those audiences were my practice audiences for everything I did later. Because there was so much love, there was never a lack of energy. It was like two hundred people were saying, *We're here for you.* You had to earn your place, for sure, and we all knew what was expected. You didn't get on the stage at the Apache unless you were ready to impress. But once we proved ourselves, it became our home base.

Later, when I went solo and released my first album, *Emotions,* I held my release party at the Apache. I'll never forget it. I had just cut my hair and gotten rid of my locks, which was a big deal. There was a poster in the club somewhere: me in a fly tan suit with a tie and brown shades...and short hair. Slick. It was like the reintroduction of PJ. I performed with Big Ed and Jesse and some other guys, of course. You didn't go to the Apache and not perform.

During those days, around 2002, I met someone at the Apache who became an invaluable part of my career: Tanya James. Initially, she was a fan, but after some conversations she started to run the merch table at our shows. Right away, I noticed how efficient Tanya was at whatever she did. Even the way she organized the tables was top-notch. When I went solo, she stayed on to help with merchandise. She was always so on top of things that I eventually made her my assistant. She was that for many years, and then, when I was without a manager, Tanya smoothly transitioned into that role. She's been my right hand ever since and I'd basically be lost without her. She keeps my life in order.

Because of everything that started there, the Apache will always be a special place for me. Even if I don't have a show, I'm gonna know somebody there. I've been chasing that same Apache vibe ever since. I want to create a scene like that for artists today. I don't know if I want a physical venue or just a traveling open mic, but I want something.

That would be me giving back. That's my reasonable service. Who's going to give new artists a platform to be seen and heard if I don't? Where would I be if the Apache hadn't done it for me? Doing something like that would be work, but it would be satisfying, too.

~

Playing the Apache was pure joy, but it was also a commercial strategy. Freestyle Nation couldn't afford radio airplay. Getting on the radio is expensive. You have to hire a radio promoter, who goes to all the major stations and plugs your song to get the hosts to play it. If you're lucky, you get a hit single. If you're not, you waste tens of thousands of dollars. We couldn't play that game, but that was okay. Playing live gave us a passionate, growing fan base.

Sadly, nothing that good lasts forever. Things started to fall apart in the summer of 2003, not long after Ruben Studdard won the second season of *American Idol*. Ruben was Cornbread's best friend; they knew each other from a Birmingham band called Just a Few Cats. After he won *American Idol* and started to tour and build his career, Ruben asked Cornbread to become his music director. I took Cornbread aside and said, "What we're building is a career, and it'll be ours. If you go out as Ruben's music director, that's just your job, and that's gonna be your job until the job is over."

Well, I tried. Cornbread took the job, and that was the beginning of the end of Freestyle Nation. It was just as well, I suppose. I'm such a workaholic that if you're not matching my intensity, I've got to go. When Lili went off to divinity school, that was the final nail in the coffin. I was adrift, wondering what to do next. College was finished. Freestyle Nation was finished. I wasn't sure what to do next. I wanted to write and work on an album of my own music, but I wasn't sure how to make that happen.

Fortunately, fate intervened. My friend Gino, who gave me that first cassette of Stevie Wonder and Donny Hathaway, was working as Erykah Badu's music director and he invited me to join her on her *Worldwide Underground Tour Part II*. She needed a keyboard player who could sing, and I could do both. I was also a huge fan. Badu is a great artist and a total professional, so of course I said yes. I had never been on tour—in fact, I had never even been on a tour bus. All of it was new.

So I left Atlanta and Freestyle Nation behind and went on tour. I was excited. I wanted to have this brand-new experience and live in the moment and write songs for the album I was working on in my head. But I was also relieved, because I thought going to college would take me out of contention for music jobs and slow my career roll. I had wanted to go to college, but that's not a musician thing unless you go to music school. Most of my friends went on tour or started gigging when they turned eighteen. I was the one who kept having to tell people, "No, I can't tour, I'm in school." When I got the call for Badu, I knew I hadn't missed the bus, literally.

I flew to Dallas, where Badu lives and her band was based, to rehearse. She was already a huge artist, but she took the time to tell me, "If you need anything, let me know." Everybody was that way, super welcoming and helpful. The musicians talked about whether to get paid directly or use an LLC so the IRS wouldn't take taxes out and that sort of thing. There was so much I didn't know, but the longer I stayed, the more I learned.

Finally, the tour started and our first show was at the House of Blues in New Orleans—home base for me. The trouble was the outfits. Man, the outfits. The vibe for the tour was the 1970s, and that meant wearing seventies bell bottoms and these long, shiny shirts. I loved seventies singer-songwriters, but I didn't want to dress like one! But then we started with a song by Larry Graham from Sly and the Family Stone, and it just...worked.

Being on tour with Badu was eye-opening. For one thing, a tour with someone that big has a lot of moving parts. I still have a photo of the list of tour personnel, and it included two personal assistants, two nutritionists, a chef, and a lot of terrific players. But being on tour was also an adjustment. For one thing, on Sundays, I didn't know if I was supposed to go to church or what. It was literally the first time I could do whatever I wanted, because even through college, I always played at churches on Sundays. That was my job. Now I was twenty-three and out on the road with a major recording artist and her band. It was liberating.

I played keys, of course, but Badu also had me on electric guitar. I played strings and auxiliary sounds and sang background vocals. But one of the most unforgettable moments was when she performed her song "In Love with You" and I accompanied her on acoustic guitar and sang it as a duet with her. Every night, it was just Badu and me, center stage. I remember being at a sold-out Radio City Music Hall, playing that song. I could barely believe it. *I'm at Radio City, it's sold out, and I'm center stage, doing a song.* Just me and Badu, in the spotlight, the entire place hushed except for our voices and the squeaking my fingers made when I moved them on the frets. It was an honor to be up there.

Later in the tour we did *David Letterman*, which was my first time doing TV. We performed Badu's new single, "Back in the Day (Puff)," but what I remember most is how cold the theater was. We got paid by the Screen Actors Guild, which was new. We performed at the end of the show, but we only did three minutes of the song, which was new. And just like that, I "caught up" with my friends who had been touring and recording while I'd been going to Morehouse and doing Freestyle Nation.

Just watching Erykah Badu command an audience was like attending a master class in being a professional and performing live. I opened up for her in Dallas and Houston in 2023, and she can still command a crowd like nobody else. She uses banter that makes people laugh while she makes them think, and her transitions between songs are perfect. She's got this trick with a drum machine that she uses to break up the monotony. She's created a hundred tricks for performing live that have become a blueprint for the rest of us. I watched and memorized everything she did. *I could use that in my shows. Maybe I won't do that. That's not my personality. But that, yeah.* She's an amazing performer. She taught me that if you build an audience, you can always go on tour and be successful. That's what I've spent years doing, and she's one of the reasons I'm able to do it.

One problem: I had writer's block! I couldn't write a word or a note. I wanted to be inspired by being out on the road, but I couldn't write anything. I became more and more frustrated until I finally realized that the best remedy was to stop worrying about writing and just take it all in. Meanwhile, I connected with a group of awesome musicians. This group called Floetry started opening for us in Houston, and they had Thaddaeus Tribbett on bass, George "Spanky" McCurdy on drums, the late Parris Bowens, one of my great friends, on keys, and my man Jeff Bradshaw on trombone. I linked up with all of them. I had my eye on producing my first solo record after the tour ended, and I was starting to put together my team of talents to paint what I wanted to paint.

Something else happened on tour that seemed small but was a sign of things to come. I've talked about how I trust my instincts when it comes to music, and how that extends to people, like me hiring Jesse to play guitar for Freestyle Nation even though I'd never heard him play. One night, these two girls tried to sneak into the Badu show with their violins. Coincidentally, I had been thinking about how much I wanted live strings on my next project. That's what I heard on the records that I loved, from the Beatles' "Eleanor Rigby" to Stevie Wonder's "Overjoyed." I just didn't know how to do it, when suddenly these two violinists fell into my lap. Security kicked them out, but I ran after them and one of them stopped to talk with me.

I said, "Hey, y'all play violin, right? I'm gonna work on an album after this tour, and I want strings." I had never heard this girl play, but I knew I had to have her on my record. Later she tried to send me a tape, and told her, "It's fine. I don't need that. I just need you. I can figure it out. I can mold your sound to what I need."

Her name was Stephanie Matthews, and she's become a star in her own right. In 2020, she put together an all-Black, all-female orchestra to play for Lizzo's opening performance at the Grammys. She played at the 2022 Academy Awards, putting together the ensemble for Beyoncé's performance of "Be Alive," from the movie *King Richard*.

I didn't know her, and she had never arranged strings, but we formed a friendship right then and there. She was finishing her degree at Indiana University, and after the tour I brought her to Atlanta to work on my first album, *Emotions*.

~

I recorded *Emotions* in 2004 at Dogwood Recording in Conyers, Georgia, and Namesake Studios in Atlanta. It was the first time I got to say, "These are my ideas. This is how I hear that. We're going to do it this way."

As soon as I got off the Erykah Badu tour, my writer's block disappeared. All these songs started to come to me. I made full demos of them using tracks, and they sounded fantastic—like full songs, only a little rawer. Keyon Harrold, a brilliant trumpeter-vocalist-composer-producer-bandleader I met on tour with Badu, told me once, "Man, those demos are almost better than the album." He was right. I always feel like songs lose something from the demo to recording them for real, because you're trying to make them perfect. D'Angelo says the same thing about his demos. There's a kind of raw energy that gets lost and that I'm always trying to recapture.

Once I got those ideas down as MP3s, the songs were basically formed. Using the vocals I had already recorded for the demos, Ron Benner, my engineer, and I started to build the rhythm tracks. It was just the two of us to start. I'm a loner in the studio, because I'm hypersensitive to people's reactions. Even if I see that you love a song, it makes me uncomfortable.

Once the tracks were done, I brought in the band. Because *Emotions* was my record, I was able to recruit everybody I loved, and I had a clear vision of whose style fit which song. I had Keyon on trumpet. He's played with everybody, and we both loved Roy Hargrove, the trumpet player on D'Angelo's album *Voodoo*. That's why *Emotions* has layers of trumpets on it. I had Cornbread from Freestyle Nation, and Darrell Freeman, who was supposed to be in my first band, on bass. I reunited with Jesse Bond on guitar. I had Brien Andrews, one of my favorite drummers from Atlanta, along with my boy Big Ed Clark. I had Stephanie on violin along with another violinist, Shelby Latin, and Colle Latin on cello. I played keys and sang lead vocals on most of the thirteen tracks (plus two bonus tracks).

I had already sent the players my demos, so when I got the players for a specific song in the studio, we just started recording it live. I don't do a lot of takes, because I like a little bit of imperfection on a recording. I want a little bit of that raw, organic demo feel. If a take feels good, I won't do more. On *Emotions*, it usually took us about three takes to get in the groove.

When I'm in the studio, I'm also trying to communicate different things than when I play a song live. You can do things live that you can't do in the studio, but when we're in the studio, I want us to feel like we're creating this unique thing. The studio is a tool where I can use delays and effects or dial in different sounds and flavors of any instrument, like Darrell's bass. That's the part where it feels like I'm a kid in a candy store. That's when it's fun.

Stephanie, Shelby, and Colle came in after to stack string parts, and Keyon came in to lay down layers of horns. I did the lead and backing vocals last, recording at a garage studio I built at the house I bought after college. I recorded at home because back then I was self-conscious about cutting vocals. I didn't even want my engineer in the room, because I might sing something that worked in context but was weird, and I knew if I saw Ron make a face I might start second-guessing my choices.

While making that record, I also saw what a true professional could do. I did a duet called "Fly Away" with gospel singer Anaysha Figueroa. I flew Anaysha into Atlanta, brought her into my home studio, and she nailed the song on the *first take*. It was incredible. It took five minutes. But I had her for the whole day, so what were we supposed to do now? I just started adding stuff, and we did another take so it wouldn't seem like I was wasting her time.

We were kids, all of us. For some of us, *Emotions* was our first album, and it was fun because I always went too far. Nobody did what I was doing. Nobody flew string players into Atlanta for their first record, not without a label behind them. But I did it. I didn't know what I couldn't do, so I did whatever I wanted.

After we finished, Ron went into the studio and started mixing the record. He got it to a certain place, and then I started adjusting, getting more of some sounds and less of others. Eventually, we got it to that right place and the file went off to mastering. We recorded between March and May 2004 and then the record came out in October 2004.

I was off and running.

Chapter Eight

Never Be the Same

Now I had a great record, but I still had a lot to learn about the music business. No label expressed any interest in signing me, which I couldn't understand. The response of fans at my live shows told me the music was great, and I thought that was all that mattered. Looking back, I realize I was a "tweener," someone whose music didn't fit into one specific genre.

Labels want hits, so they're comfortable when they can put you in a category: R&B, gospel, hip-hop, and so on. My songs weren't sexual enough to be R&B, and they definitely weren't gospel. I had created my own genre, PJ Morton, so nobody knew how much interest there would be in buying my record, and they didn't know how to market me. I was stuck in the middle with nobody willing to take a risk.

I didn't care about hits or fitting into a category. To be fair, a part of me did want a major label to tell me, "PJ, we see what you're doing and we love it. Here's a contract!" Anybody who says they don't crave a little of that validation is lying. However, with

Emotions, I was finally speaking with my true artistic voice, and I wanted to keep making music that fit my vision. I didn't want some record executive telling me what to write or how to produce. That meant taking the path of an independent artist. The trouble was, back then I didn't understand how the independent world worked, either.

I had been reading about how Dave Matthews had built his following, and I thought I knew what I was doing. iTunes had launched in 2001 and Myspace had gone live in 2003, so I had some tools. I could use the Internet to find out where my people lived and where they were buying my CDs. But to really make *Emotions* successful, I needed to go on tour. I knew if I could play in front of my fans, they would support what I was doing. Playing live would be my substitute for radio.

A lot of acts don't translate well to live performance. But Freestyle Nation shows at the Apache and other venues had shown me that fans *loved* the way my songs sounded live. If we had CDs, they bought them. They told their friends. They came to every show and sold out every room. That's intentional. When I write, I'm always thinking about how a song will translate to live performance. Ever wonder why I write a lot of choruses that repeat the same phrase over and over? I do it because those choruses are easy for an audience to sing along with. That's a pop music concept I've adapted to soul.

Ever since the House of Blues, I had focused on putting together great live shows. When I put out *Emotions*, I looked around the music business and saw a lot of acts that didn't seem to put much effort into putting on a great live show. That made my shows my biggest competitive advantage. I knew my band and I knew we could pack venues.

Now I just had to figure out how to pay for a tour. Without a label, I would have to pay for travel, equipment, and hotels, and pay my band, all out of my own pocket. I was prepared to go without pay myself so I could bring a big group on the road—Big Ed, Brian, my own horn section—and have the big sound I loved. If I was gonna do this, I would do it right.

Fortunately, when I wasn't playing live, rehearsing, or in the studio, I was working as a songwriter and producer with Jermaine Dupri. I was also working with major artists like Monica, Jagged Edge, and LL Cool J, refining my skills as a producer and a songwriter, building relationships in the music industry, and getting paid. That work paid off when I signed a six-figure publishing deal with Famous Music Corporation, the music publishing division of Paramount Pictures.

Famous Music would own the rights to the songs I wrote for Jermaine or other producers, and I would be obligated to write a certain number of songs during the life of the contract, but I would get a share of the royalties those songs earned along with money up front. It was huge. I took the bulk of my advance and my band and I went on the road to promote *Emotions*.

But this was not an Erykah Badu tour. We couldn't afford a tour bus on my budget. Instead, I asked my mom if I could borrow the charter bus that she used for her women's ministry, Women of Excellence. She said yes, and a few weeks later we started pulling up to clubs in the South in a purple, pink, and white church bus. People were doing double takes in the parking lot and probably thinking, *What is a women's conference doing coming to this club?*

That was the start of the *Emotions* OG (Official Grind) tour. I brought a fourteen-piece band complete with my own horn section, and club operators had never seen anything like it. We played the Apache, of course, but no promoters knew who I was, so we had to handle all our own bookings. We played thirteen or fourteen venues from Birmingham to Charleston, and even played a party somewhere down in Florida. Like a barnstorming baseball team from the 1930s, we played everywhere and anywhere we could draw a crowd.

I told promoters, "Just pay us on the door," which they were happy to do. I wasn't worried, because I was confident that we could draw crowds. We'd pull audiences of one hundred to two hundred people most nights (we had a few duds where only twenty people showed, but not many), and they would be singing along with every song, just like at the Apache. A big, engaged crowd makes a great live show, and it also makes it easier to get bookings even if you're unsigned. The owners and promoters knew that when we came to town, we could fill their rooms, show their guests a great time, and make them money. That landed us bookings that a lot of other unsigned artists couldn't get.

Touring for *Emotions* was also a crash course in the music business. It showed me that if I wanted to get my fans to come out and see me play, I had to focus on building my live audience. Having followers on social media isn't the same as having fans who will come out and see you live. I know artists with millions of Instagram followers who can't fill the venues that I play, because they haven't cultivated that fan base. If you want someone to see you live, you have to make them want to buy a ticket, leave their house, drive to a venue, find parking, and wait in line. You have to make sure they know they'll have an experience they can't have by listening to your music on Spotify. I worked hard to make that happen.

Still, *Emotions* didn't chart, have a single, or get radio airplay. Failure? Not to me. It was my first chance to produce music my way, organize and run a tour, build an audience, start my family of musicians, and build a network of club operators. I was a little frustrated that I couldn't get any label interest, but looking back, I was lucky a label didn't offer me a deal in 2005, because I would've taken it.

Back then, there was no path for someone like me to build a successful career. None of my heroes had gone big by being independent. Prince was with Warner Records before he started Paisley Park. Stevie was with Motown for most of his career. I was just putting one foot in front of the other and making it up as I went. But I was also learning how to assemble a band, organize a tour, build an audience, and develop a sound that reflected my true voice. If I'd been signed, I might have compromised to have a hit. I would've had to play the numbers game.

Ironically, by the end of the tour, I started to get calls from small labels interested in signing me. *No, thanks.* I wasn't ready yet. Signed artists had to conform to a system. Not me. I didn't have to answer to anybody but myself. I knew that, someday, that would probably change. If the right offer came at the right time, I might sign. But at that time, I was content being independent.

~

But *Emotions* wasn't the big news of 2005. It was Hurricane Katrina. By that summer, the tour was over. I was living in Atlanta producing records and commuting to New Orleans on the weekends to help my dad as music director at the church. I wasn't ready to leave Atlanta, because I was still working in the industry and building my professional network, so every Saturday night I would fly to New Orleans, and then on Wednesday I'd fly back home.

A few days before Katrina hit, we could all see that it was going to be a terrible storm and that it was tracking directly for the city. My flight to New Orleans for Saturday, August 27, was canceled. The next day, Sunday, one day before the storm made landfall, my family evacuated. My dad held church services and then he, my mom, and my sisters flew to New Jersey, where my dad was scheduled to preach, and then to Atlanta.

Because I had a house in Atlanta, my family came and stayed with me. It all seemed like a bad dream until we watched news coverage of the storm. Even before Katrina made landfall at about 6:00 a.m. on Monday, August 29, it sent a fifteen-foot storm surge up the Mississippi River, overwhelming the levees that protected so many areas from flooding. New Orleans East, where I had grown up, was submerged under flood waters. The lower floor of my parents' new house, where they had moved after I left for college, was flooded with eight feet of water. Neighborhoods like the Lower Ninth Ward, Gentilly, and Lakeview were devastated. Thousands of residents were trapped, and many more were displaced as they were forced to leave the city. The community, history, and heritage of the city I loved, the city that shaped me, looked like it was gone forever.

My dad landed on his feet as best he could. To the tens of thousands of people in his congregation, he was a leader, and those people were now scattered and displaced, many of them sheltering with family and friends in Atlanta while they tried to figure out what to do next. So he started a new church in Atlanta to serve the displaced members of Greater St. Stephen.

It might seem strange that he didn't go back to New Orleans to minister to the people there, but you have to understand that at the time there wasn't much of New Orleans to go back to.

Practically every neighborhood and every building had suffered damage, and many of the people from the Greater St. Stephen community had washed up in Atlanta without any idea of when they would go home...or *if* they would go home.

Many had lost everything, and even the ones who hadn't lost their homes were confused and grieving, worried about family members, friends, and the future. The new church gave them a place to come together, reconnect, and find hope. That was what they needed, and that's why Dad saw the need to start a new church.

First, the church was located in Decatur, Georgia, about seven miles outside Atlanta. Then Tyler Perry came into the picture. He and my father went in together to buy the land for the new Atlanta church. The church was on one side of the property, and Tyler's first movie backlot was on the other side. This was before he bought the 330 acres that became Tyler Perry Studios.

When the new church was completed, my dad named it Changing a Generation. It became a home away from home for so many displaced people in Atlanta. I handled the music, which was another full circle moment for me. I had left New Orleans to put some distance between myself and the church, and here I was, back with my dad at church.

But before long, we had to deal with what had happened to New Orleans. We had all seen the news coverage: people being evacuated on boats and sheltering in the Superdome, the streets filled with debris and sewage. My dad went back to the city several times in the fall, and in November 2005 I went with him. On the drive west, I tried not to think about what we might find, but when we finally arrived, it was worse than I could have imagined.

New Orleans was like a ghost town. I had never seen the city not alive with people, color, and music, but this place looked like a set from the Will Smith movie *I Am Legend*. Even three months later, debris was everywhere. Entire districts had been wiped out. There was nobody in the streets, and in New Orleans, there had always been people in the streets. The apartment where my stuff was, and where I stayed when I commuted, had been destroyed. Ultrasonic Studios, where I had first seen music produced as a child, was wrecked and never rebuilt. My city had been blown apart. It was just...bleak.

My dad, however, was on a mission. Most of the folks from Greater St. Stephen had gotten out of the city, and many of them were in Atlanta, but he knew that a few were still in New Orleans. When we were in Atlanta, his thought was, *Who is serving them? We need to get back. We need to make sure.* Many congregations had been displaced, and many pastors were trying to keep things going as best they could in the cities they had landed in. But my dad was aware of his position as a leader in the church and his role as the shepherd of his flock. He knew he had to set the example, so he became one of the first pastors to return to the city after the hurricane. He was trying his best to find his people and make sure they were okay.

Not long after that, he and my mom started commuting between Atlanta and New Orleans—ministering to Changing a Generation, and then flying back to lead services at Greater St. Stephen. Where did they stay in a ruined city? The lower floor of their house had been destroyed by floodwaters, but the upper floor was dry, and that's where most of their furniture was, so they lived there.

As strange as it was to be back in New Orleans, it was almost as surreal to be in Atlanta with all the New Orleans people who were out of place. Basically, New Orleans had migrated east, and everybody was disoriented. Nobody knew what they were doing. FEMA was giving out credits for hotels, and some of my friends went from hotel to hotel trying to find a FEMA hotel. Some people even flashed the vouchers at five-star hotels. Some were cool and said, "Okay, we'll allow you to stay here for a week," but I couldn't help wondering what everybody was going to do in the long term. How long was this going to last?

FEMA also gave displaced people $2,000 to cover basic living expenses, and some folks thought that money was going to last forever. I saw some of them in the mall buying designer clothes, and I wanted to take them aside and say, *I don't know if you guys realize this, but that money may have to stretch for a while.* I don't think anybody had any idea how big the aftermath of Katrina was or how long it would last. We all thought people would be back home in two weeks, but some people were still displaced after two *years.* The only thing I knew was that everything was going to be different from then on. I was just trying to figure out what to do next.

~

It took a long time for New Orleans to recover. I think what was missed the most were the local people. When I went back with my dad, the only people I saw were aid workers and construction crews demolishing flooded buildings and cleaning up fence boards, roof shingles, jagged pieces of concrete, and other debris. For me, what makes New Orleans special is being able to walk down the street and say "Hey" to a stranger. That was gone. That's what I was missing.

In the last few years, I think that's finally come back. The people of New Orleans are back. I feel like my home is back, too. It's taken twenty years, because it's not just about people moving back into their old neighborhoods. It's about them feeling like they're home. That means rebuilding homes, but it also means giving people a sense of safety.

Greater St. Stephen didn't survive Katrina undamaged. The hurricane caused severe flood damage to the Uptown church, and three years later, a fire destroyed the building. All these years later, it's still being rebuilt. My sister Jasmine and her husband now lead Greater St. Stephen in New Orleans East. My dad was supposed to retire in 2020, but the pandemic happened and messed up his succession plan.

My dad has always done things his own way, and his retirement was no exception. He's the only pastor I ever heard say he planned to retire at a young age. "I'm retiring at sixty-five. The way people retire," he would say. He didn't want to be one of those pastors who stay in the pulpit until they can no longer function. Then when he was fifty-five, Katrina happened, and he had a brand-new church to start in Atlanta. The year after that, he was diagnosed with colon cancer, though after treatment he's been cancer-free. Retirement had to wait.

But nobody's tougher than my dad. In 2006, he put out a new record, *Still Standing*, which was his defiant response to Katrina. That same year, he delivered an incredible performance at GSS, where he sang the title song, "I'm Still Standing," for nearly ten minutes in front of a praising full house.

At that service he told the congregation, "I appreciate, all over this world, people praying for me. I've been through a whole lot. But I've come to let you know tonight that in the midst of it all... I'm still standing!"

So is New Orleans. And in 2021, my dad was finally able to retire.

Chapter Nine

New Orleans Girl

Before Katrina, I had my own personal disaster: a big, ugly, very public breakup. I had been engaged to a well-known New Orleans radio personality. Because she was a public figure, and I was Bishop Paul Morton's son, everybody knew about us, which made it even more embarrassing when things fell apart.

We split for a lot of reasons. I was just twenty-three, and she was seven years older than me. Also, bad things that had happened in her life broke her ability to trust people, especially me. I was flying into New Orleans every week to help my dad at church, then flying back to Atlanta on Wednesdays, but every Wednesday seemed to turn into an argument. What was I doing on my own in Atlanta? Was I behaving? Was I seeing someone else? Eventually, to my relief, the whole thing just fell apart.

Around that time, Kortni came back into my life. I had known her since we were kids. She's a minister's daughter, and her brother and I were junior deacons in Greater St. Stephen, so she and I grew up together. But we went our own ways as adults and I hadn't seen her in a while. Around the time of my breakup, she had gotten pregnant out of wedlock—a huge taboo in the church world. But it was my mom's birthday and I was back in New Orleans to celebrate, and I went to the church for an event. Then I looked around and saw Kortni sitting in the back.

I walked over and sat down near her. We were both in a bad place—her because of the pregnancy, me because of my very public breakup—and we needed to be in a nonjudgmental space for a while. We just started talking, and it was the first time she and I had ever had a real conversation. After a while she made a joke and I thought, *Okay, she's cool.* She had always been good friends with my little sister, Christiann, so I figured she had to be a cool person.

I didn't want another relationship, though. I just wanted to be her friend. Still, on that day in the church, we bonded over being outcasts, and later on, we started to date and hang out a little bit in New Orleans, but nothing super serious. Then in November 2004, her son Jakai was born.

Little Jakai. He was such a cute kid, but I didn't really engage with him early on. I still didn't know if it was going to be serious between me and Kortni, and I thought I should keep my distance. Then in 2005, Katrina happened and everything changed. FEMA was moving people all over the place, and out of all the places they could have relocated Kortni and Jakai, they put them in an apartment one mile from my house in Atlanta. We had lived in the same apartment complex in New Orleans, but this seemed like a sign.

At that point, our relationship started to get more serious, and I started to spend more time with Jakai. I'd go over to see her, but end up spending most of my time playing with him. I had never thought of myself as a father, and I had never dated a girl with a kid before. That was a first. I didn't see being an instant dad as part of my path. But as always, life is full of surprises.

Maybe it was my dad's example, but some hidden fatherly instincts kicked in. I thought, *If I'm going to be around this much, I want to make sure Jakai is taken care of.* I started spending more time with him and taking him to nursery school. I never treated him like my stepson, and he's never called me his stepdad. He's my son, and I've been "Dad" since I took him to Chuck E. Cheese for his second birthday.

The only bad part about that day was that I took him to the *wrong* Chuck E. Cheese. We were both happy and excited for the birthday party, and I just assumed we were having the party at the same Chuck E. Cheese we always went to. As I was driving there, I felt so proud. This was me by myself, being a dad. I didn't really do dad things without Kortni, but Jakai had called me "Dad" that day for the first time and I didn't want to tell him not to. We pulled up to Chuck E. Cheese and went inside, ready to party... and we couldn't find any of the families we'd invited. Jakai was supposed to be the star of the show, but there was no show.

I had to call Kortni and say, "Honey, I think I went to the wrong Chuck E. Cheese." Very patiently, she gave me the correct address, and then I turned to my little guy and said, "Man, I'm sorry, but we're at the wrong one." He was so cool about it; he was always my little buddy that way. We got back in the car and drove to the right location. It was a little adventure and one of our first bonding moments.

At the end of 2005, I enrolled Jakai in The Suzuki School, an incredibly selective, expensive Montessori school in suburban Atlanta. It cost more than I could afford, but I wanted to take on that responsibility. It felt right. I think that development at an early age put him on the right path, because he's been a great student ever since.

~

During that time, I was thinking about proposing to Kortni, but I didn't. Having already had one engagement fall apart, the idea of proposing again was traumatic. Thankfully, Kortni wasn't in a rush, which was a good thing, because right around the end of 2007, we broke up. I don't remember why. I don't remember anything bad happening. I did know that no matter what happened, I would take care of Jakai. I would be "Uncle PJ" if I had to be.

I started seeing this other girl I liked who lived in Louisiana, and one day, on my way back from Louisiana to Atlanta, I got stopped by a cop for speeding on Interstate 10 outside of Baton Rouge. Backstory: I had already gotten several speeding tickets, and the Atlanta court had suspended my license. Before I left Atlanta to see this girl, I paid about one thousand dollars to get the suspension lifted. What I didn't know was that I was supposed to take that receipt to another office, where they would officially lift the suspension. I didn't do that, so as I was driving back to Atlanta, my license was still suspended.

The officer pulled me over, I handed him my license, and he ran it. All of a sudden, he was at my window, his hand on his sidearm, barking, "Get out of the car and put your hands behind your back!" I was stunned. I said, "Officer, there's got to be a mistake. I literally just paid a thousand dollars a couple of days ago. I know it's not suspended."

He ordered me out of the car again. I put my hands behind my back, and he cuffed me, put me in the back of his police car, and took me to jail. The officer led me inside, and the first thing I saw was a guy going crazy. The guards had him in what's known as a "prison wrap" so he couldn't injure himself, but it was an unnerving thing to see. I had never been arrested, and I had no idea what was going to happen. I was booked and had my possessions taken, and then a guard took me to a holding cell. It was packed with a bunch of guys sitting around the perimeter on benches, all muttering things like, "I knew I shouldn't have done that" and "I knew I was about to get caught." These were the DUIs, the drug possession busts, and the guys arrested for stealing copper wire out of a house.

I just sat there, not saying anything. They brought food for breakfast, but I couldn't eat. A few hours later lunch came, but I wasn't hungry. My mind was racing. *How do I get out of here? Who can I call? What's going to happen?* There was a pay phone on the wall inside the cell with numbers for bail bondsmen posted nearby (we weren't allowed to use cell phones). The problem was that they had confiscated my phone and one of the few numbers I knew from memory was for Ed's old house, where his mom, Mrs. Gloria, still lived.

I called. Answering machine.

The only other thing I could think of to do was to call a bail bondsman and ask him if he would call my friend, Sheldon, because I also knew Sheldon's cell phone number. I called one of the numbers on the wall, and the bail bondsman was—well, let's just say shady characters probably call him all the time. He said, "Look, if your friend doesn't use us, we're not going to have him call you back." But I had no choice. He said he'd call Sheldon and hung up. I went back into my cell.

They passed out dinner: cookies and a rock hard sandwich. Stupidly, I said, "Hey, anybody want my sandwich? I'm just going to eat the cookies." This dude sitting next to me said, "Hey, man, I'm right here. Why you ain't asking me if I want your sandwich?" I put my head in my hands and thought, *I've got to get out of here.*

But I also thought about the girl I had gone to see, and it was suddenly crystal clear that she wasn't who I wanted. I *knew* who I wanted. That night, Sheldon picked me up, thank God, and I spent the night at his house. Driving back to Atlanta the next morning—being very careful to observe the speed limit—I made a decision. If I went back to Kortni, I had to propose. I didn't want to ramp up to it. I was all in.

When I got back, I took a few days to find the right ring and have it designed, and then I drove to the natural hair salon where she worked. I called her from the parking lot and asked her to walk out and meet me. Kortni's really shy and I didn't want to make my proposal a spectacle. When she came out, she wasn't sure what was happening. After all, we were still broken up. I was sitting in my car, and when she got in the other seat, I handed her a box. Inside it was a cheap necklace, which I intended as a sort of decoy. She looked at me, confused, and said, "What is this?"

Then I showed her the ring. She couldn't believe it. The first thing she said was, "That's not real." Then I said, "Will you marry me?" Her eyes went wide, and she said, "You didn't even let me get my nails done!" That will go down in history as the first thing my wife said to me when I proposed. But she hugged me and kissed me and said yes. Then she went back into the salon . . . and the place went crazy. Every woman in there started screaming.

It was a sweet moment.

~

People don't always see Kortni's shyness at first because her style is . . . definitely not shy. She has a crazy sense of fashion; it's one of the things that drew me to her. But if you don't know her, you might think she's outgoing. Interviewers will ask her questions and she'll start sweating. Before we dated, her face was always so set, and she was so quiet, I thought she was mean. (She won't be mad at me for writing that; she knows it and we laugh about it.)

When I finally had a conversation with Kortni, I found out that she's the sweetest person in the world. She's not going to initiate a conversation; she's too shy for that. But she's incredibly caring, a great listener, and really easy to talk to, which are some of the reasons I love her. After my bad breakup, when we started talking in the back of the church, I didn't feel any pressure. She felt like a safe place to me, and she still does.

Kortni and my sister Christiann have been tight for years. When we announced our engagement, my sister took me aside and said sweetly, "If you hurt her, I'll kill you." So I thought it best not to waste a lot of time. After all, we'd already waited four years. But now we had to navigate big pressure from the GSS community. Everybody who had ever babysat me or listened to me sing on Sunday expected an invitation to our wedding. When you're the preacher's kid, your extended family is the whole church. But I dreaded the idea of a big, stressful wedding. My sister Jasmine had two thousand people at her wedding along with fourteen brides-maids and groomsmen. They took up the whole church. It was like Prince William marrying Kate Middleton.

Thankfully, Kortni didn't want a big wedding, either, so we picked Christmas Day as our date. We figured most folks would be with their families, letting us keep things small and simple. We got married at my parents' house and ended up having seventy-five guests. My guy Jakai was the ring bearer, and my friend Kenneth was my best man. Because it was December, we had the ceremony indoors, by the piano that I'd learned on with Mr. Alphonse all those years before. I played a song I'd written for Kortni called "Here for You."

Christiann designed everything—the decorations, the invitations—and made it all simple, classy, and beautiful. She's always been the most creative one in our family; there seems to be nothing she can't do. Jasmine sings, I sing and play, and I'll draw a little bit, but Christy does it all. She's a graphic artist. She's a singer. She's a makeup artist. She actually can't figure out what she wants to do for a career because she can do so many things so well. She reminds me of my mother because she's a dreamer and has almost too many ideas to contain. But that day, her ideas brought every-thing together.

It was a perfect day.

When I talked to Jasmine afterward, she said, "You had my dream wedding. I don't even remember my wedding. I had noth-ing to do with it." That's that first kid thing again, wanting to please everybody. Kortni and I wanted to please ourselves.

Now we lived together in Atlanta, and I was a dad. It was my childhood dream to have twins—what young boy prays for twins?—and when Kortni got pregnant with twins in 2009, it felt like God had answered that prayer. Then she lost them at twenty weeks and still had to go through labor because she was so far along. We cried together, but we healed together, too.

In 2010, she was pregnant again, and things got a little crazy. I was on tour, playing the tree-lighting ceremony at the White House and hoping I would get to meet President Obama. After the ceremony, I got to shake his hand, and then I took the late train from DC to New York so I could play what was then called *Late Night with Jimmy Fallon* the next day. While I was on that train, Kortni went into labor.

While she and Christiann rushed to the hospital in Atlanta, I tried to get a flight home. We weren't at the private plane level yet, and I couldn't get a commercial flight until 6:00 a.m. the next day. So I stayed up all night in my hotel room, watching the birth of my son Paul Morton III (I call him P3) on FaceTime. I had great WiFi, so the picture and sound were perfect. P3 wasn't in a hurry, but at around 3:00 in the morning, after hours of labor, Kortni gave a last push and then I heard my son cry for the first time. I jumped on the plane the next morning and was in Atlanta by 7:30.

Everybody at the hospital was waiting for me, and when I got there, they took me straight into the room. Kortni was still in bed, looking tired but happy, so I went over and kissed her. My dad smothered me with a hug. He looked so proud, and I knew what part of that was about. *Now there is a boy who will carry on my name.* I think that was a big deal for him. Then Kortni handed me my boy. My namesake, wrapped up in blankets. He was beautiful, already with a head full of curly hair, and he looked at me like he already knew who I was. I think I was a little bit in shock. *I did this, I made a life.* Later that day, the whole family came to the hospital, and it was a celebration. I never did play *Fallon*.

Two years later, I made sure I was in the room when Peyton was born. She was born in Los Angeles, and that birth was much smoother. She was also born the day after Christmas, so things were quiet. I was in the hospital room with Kortni, and it was too late for her to get an epidural, because Peyton was coming quick. Before I knew it, there she was, my little girl. A few minutes later, Jakai walked in the room and immediately burst out crying. P3 was just two years old, too little to know what was happening, but they were both happy to have a little sister.

As soon as Peyton popped out, I knew I was done. I thought, *My family is complete.* I had grown up in a family of two girls and one boy. Now I had two boys and one girl. The symmetry was perfect. We didn't find out the gender of our baby when Kortni was pregnant with P3, and even though we did with Peyton, Kortni didn't believe it. She knew I wanted a girl and she was worried she was going to have another boy. Then when Peyton came out, we looked at each other and just knew. *This feels complete.*

I had my daddy's girl, and believe me, there's nothing I wouldn't do for her. We throw "I love yous" to each other all day long. While I was working on this book, I walked sixteen thousand steps in a Mardi Gras parade. That was basically a meet and greet for me in New Orleans, because people were saying, "What on earth is PJ Morton doing in the street?" Being a chaperone for my daughter's dance team, that's what.

I'm the "fun dad." I'm still a kid, and I don't want to grow up. I know the realities of life, but I'm successful enough where I get to be a little bit willfully ignorant and keep dreaming like when I was

a kid. When I was in South Africa, I spent time with Robert Bro-
zin, the cofounder of this restaurant chain called Nando's. This
guy is about sixty-five years old, and he walks around in sneakers
and shorts and still gets excited about new ideas.

That's going to be me at sixty-five. I never want to lose that
spirit. It keeps you young. Whatever my kids tell me, nothing
sounds crazy. My dad was the same way. He'd tell me, "All right,
genius. You got it." I think that makes me a cool dad. I give them
room for dreams and big ideas because I still think in terms of
dreams and big ideas. That makes our relationship different. I'm a
living example of what's possible, because I've done it. My dad was
that for me, so I know how powerful it is.

~

Because Kortni and I grew up in my dad's church, it feels like we've
been together forever. But we still weren't prepared for Jakai to
go to Morehouse. He's no longer a little guy. He's nearly twenty
years old now, six-one, tall, dark, and handsome, and is starting his
sophomore year at my alma mater. He's always been smart, but to
watch him grow into a man has been amazing. People are always
telling me, "Your son is so respectful," which is my favorite compliment to hear. It feels like a job well done.

He's determined about whatever he puts his mind to, so much
so that once he says, "I've got it," you can't tell him anything. He's
a double major: political science and finance with a pre-law track.
He wants to be a sports agent. To watch him grinding to do something totally different from me makes me so happy. But he still
plays the drums at a church on Sundays, so he's got his musical
side, too.

Everything really hit me when we went for our Morehouse visit in summer 2023. Jakai had been accepted, but he had to do the incoming freshman interview. The school was putting together a video compilation of sons' interviews, and another of interviews with fathers, and they asked Jakai about why he chose to go to Morehouse. He said, "My dad has always given me enough space to make my own decisions."

Listening to that, it hit me. He was describing exactly what my dad did for me. My dad respected me enough to let me make my own decisions, even when that meant turning my back on the path he had in mind for me. Once, I gave Jakai the keys to our house so he could watch his brother and sister when we weren't home; my father did the same thing with me. In raising Jakai, I had copied my father, move for move. I just hadn't realized it until that moment.

The college staff interviewed dads and sons separately, and when they came to interview me, the interviewer said, "We talked to Jakai, and the first thing he wanted to say to you was 'Thank you.'" I felt tears coming to my eyes, but I kept it together, just barely.

Chapter Ten

Thank You

I was back in Atlanta with a family to support, but I wasn't sure where to take my career. My experiences on tour had convinced me that I wasn't interested in a major label deal, but at the same time I was becoming frustrated with the limitations that came with being an independent.

I was looking for something that didn't exist at that time: creative independence and agility with the reach and marketing muscle of a major label. There were some successful independent labels in rock and pop, but not in soul music. After Motown and Chess, which were mostly doing big-time R&B, there was a gap. Dave Matthews was building a massive audience doing his own thing, but in my world, that was rare. Eric Roberson, who went by Erro, created his own label, Blue Erro Soul. Frank McComb, who worked with people like Prince, Chaka Khan, Will Smith, and Branford Marsalis, went independent in 2002 and launched his own label, Boobescoot Music, in 2005. We're all brothers, and we even did a concert together in Atlanta in 2006 called *The Kings of*

Underground Soul. But we were pretty much the only ones doing that. It was a lonely road.

Part of the problem was timing: I was too early. Spotify, iTunes, and social media existed in 2008 but weren't big enough to change the game for artists like me. The label model was still mostly about retail distribution and radio—placing CDs in stores and getting songs played on the air. Now it's all about streams and building an audience online. Technology has made it so much easier to be independent today than it was back then. I guess it was my own fault for being ahead of my time.

My uncertainty shaped my career path for a while. For several years, I had one foot in and one foot out of the business. I was still working on my own music, but I was writing and producing for top artists like Faith Evans, Monica, and gospel star Kierra Sheard. During this period, I wrote the gospel hit "Let Go" for DeWayne Woods, which won a Stellar Award. But friends in the industry said, "P, let's just get you one hit. Let's just play this hit game." I always thought that mentality was shortsighted.

People acted like if you got that one hit, you had it made. You could do whatever you wanted after that. That's not true. If you create the expectation that you can keep making hits, you can become a prisoner of that expectation. You might produce a record that's artistically brilliant, but if it doesn't have at least one song that charts, it's considered a commercial failure. So I told all those friends and colleagues that I was good. I wasn't worried about having a hit. Later, some of them came to see why I felt that way.

One of my closest friends in the business was a songwriter named LaShawn Daniels. Before he died in a car accident in 2019, he wrote for some of the biggest names in the world, including

Michael Jackson, Beyoncé, and Destiny's Child. LaShawn was one of the people who most wanted to see me have a hit. But about a year before he passed, he left LA and he started doing some of his own stuff. Later he told me, "P, now I get why you were holding off."

Hits are hard to get. You can't just create them on demand. You might write a song and think, *Yeah, this is gonna chart.* But you still have to release the song and the audience gets the final say. Sometimes they say no. By not worrying about hits, I could prioritize artistry over sales. I could play sold-out venues and sell enough CDs to recoup my costs. I didn't have to compromise my artistic voice and vision because a record executive told me my last single didn't move enough units. I also had one big advantage over a lot of independent artists: my publishing deal.

That deal was my substitute for a record deal, and it helped me with the cost of recording sessions, tour expenses, and paying my band. That allowed me to build my career blueprint. Conventional success was still tempting, not because I craved validation but because I wanted to know what I was capable of with the resources, the people, and the marketing budget of a major label behind me. Could I reach a bigger audience and move them with my ideas the way I did my live audiences? I would've loved to find out, but it was more important to me to keep my voice and vision authentic.

I decided to take the scenic route. I would build a real fan base of real people. I would make great music, play fantastic live shows, and not worry about what the major labels were doing. I could win my way, keep feeding my musicians, and make the kind of music I could be proud of.

~

That meant touring, and for several years, I had been touring consistently to support records like *Emotions* and my 2007 album, *Perfect Song*. In the process, I had built a first-class live band that was more like a family: Big Ed on drums, Jesse Bond on guitar, David Crenshaw on percussion, JoJo Martin and Zebulon Ellis on vocals, and Brian Cockerham on bass. I mention Brian last because he's my best friend, and he deserves a couple of pages here.

I didn't grow up with Brian, but his best friend, Little Larry, this short dude who could really play, was the drummer at my uncle's church, New Beginnings. I just knew Brian as an up-and-coming bass player. I lost track of him for a while, but eventually I found out that he had gone to Boston with Jesse to attend the Berklee School of Music. We reconnected when Freestyle Nation was breaking up and Cornbread was going on the road with Ruben Studdard. I needed a bass player who could fill Cornbread's shoes, and thought about Brian. He joined the band for a gig in Charleston, South Carolina, in February 2005 and he's been with me ever since.

After Katrina, I invited Brian and Big Ed to go with me to London for two weeks. My excuse was that Famous Music, my publisher, had an office there and I could set up some meetings. But mostly, I just felt a pull to London. I didn't even have any gigs set up. I wanted to write songs and see what London was all about, so I decided to take Brian and Ed with me and see what happened.

We stayed in a neighborhood right around the corner from Abbey Road Studios. Later we found a piano store down the street that had practice rooms. After that, the three of us walked around London all day, just taking it all in. We listened to the accents, learned where to look to avoid getting run over (because everybody drives on the left), and rode the Underground. Then I came back to our hotel, booked a practice room for an hour, and wrote songs.

Coffeehouse open mic nights and a soul-R&B night at a local pub gave us the chance to test out the new songs. It was an adventure and I had my boys with me, so I felt like we could do anything. When I have Brian and Ed with me, I don't care where we are. We can set up and play music.

One day, we were headed to Piccadilly Circus, one of the busiest parts of Central London, and on a whim I told Brian to wear his bass slung across his back so people would know we were musicians. My gut was telling me that something would happen. Well, it did. As soon as we got off the Tube at Piccadilly and walked up to the street, this white dude came up to us and said, "Hey, man, are you guys musicians?" He was an American from Denver, and Brian said, "We know somebody from Colorado, our friend J. Most."

The guy was blown away. "I know J. Most!" Just like that, we'd made a friend. The plan worked like a charm. There's something about musicians that attracts people.

Another time, we walked to the Nigerian restaurant across the street from our hotel to eat. The staff heard our accents and started asking, "Where are you from?" When we told them we were musicians, they went and got the owner. He came to our table and said, "I would love for you to play here, man. Can we do something? Can we set up something?" He was so excited that we said yes. This guy closed down the restaurant, set up a keyboard and some drums, and we played a private concert that night for about twenty people.

I wish I could remember the owner's name, but I know that we made friends everywhere we went and learned about the city through the eyes of the people who lived there. We just swung for the fences every day and whatever happened, happened.

The one bad part of the trip came when we bought international calling cards for the trip. Remember those? There weren't international mobile calling plans yet, so you prepaid for phone minutes on your calling card, used a special number to make calls from public phones, and you wouldn't get hit with big charges. We thought we had about thirty thousand minutes on our cards, so we used them for the entire trip, but we kept dialing the wrong number. Then we got the bill when we tried to check out. *Fourteen thousand dollars.* I don't usually raise my voice, but that was the first time Brian saw me scream. (For the record, I negotiated the bill down by about two-thirds so we could get out of London.)

Brian is one of the nicest people in the world. After we got back from London, I wanted to spend some time away from Atlanta, so I moved to the Bronx to live with Brian in his grandmother's basement, and he started showing me New York. We ran through that scene, and he took me everywhere.

He took me to Cafe Wha?, where Bob Dylan played and Jimi Hendrix and Allen Ginsberg would hang out. He took me to Bleecker Street, where all the famous Greenwich Village nightclubs were. We went to The Bitter End, where Dylan also played. I was obsessed with Bob Dylan and the world of folk and poetry, but I had no idea you could still go to all those places. I sat in The Bitter End, with its blue awning, wooden storefront, brick stage wall, and pictures of everybody from George Carlin to Simon & Garfunkel behind the bar, and watched artists play everything from folk to punk rock.

Brian even took me to the basketball court where the iconic bass player Jaco Pastorius famously hooked up his amp and played

"The Star Spangled Banner." I only lived with Brian for a year and a half, but I loved it. New York immediately accepted me, and I knew I was on the right path.

~

When you tour as an independent, you have to pay for everything out of your own pocket. By now, I knew that putting on great live shows was my calling card, so we started off with a band that was even larger than the group I tour with today. I loved the orchestral arrangements that were a big part of the Motown sound—that rich sound you can only get with a large band. So we had extra horns and extra singers.

That's how people started to know me and my sound, because I was bringing in something different from anyone else. Our shows looked like we had a major budget behind us, but we didn't. For years, I didn't pay myself a salary. I supported Kortni and Jakai with the income I made from producing and songwriting. I could have downsized the show and put money in my pocket, but presentation was more important to me than money. Plus, I needed to take care of the members of my band.

We played mostly smaller venues in front of two hundred or three hundred people. It's tough to book bigger venues if you're not signed, but it's possible if you prove that you can sell tickets. If you can sell out a three-hundred-seat club, you can talk to bigger venues, sell more tickets, and make more money. That's one of the free-market parts of the business I appreciate.

Touring and playing live also let me know that even though I didn't have a major label deal, I still had hits. At any of my shows, I could look into the audience and see people in the front row singing every word of every song. If that's not having a hit, I don't know what is.

It also felt good to have my friends working instead of having to take side gigs to make rent. My band and I have been together a long time, and they're family. Brian's been with me for seventeen years, Big Ed for more than twenty years. My horn players, percussionists, backup singers…they're my people. I'm responsible for them. It's up to me to keep them working. I love seeing Ed be able to take care of his family with what he earns as a professional drummer. It's a source of pride for me to be able to take care of other musicians.

That hasn't changed from 2008 to today. If you go backstage at any of my shows, you'll find the happiest, tightest group of musicians you've ever seen. One of the people who I've known the longest is my background singer, Jarell Bankston. I met Jarell in high school in New Orleans, when he was a phenom among New Orleans singers. He's always been a techie, so people knew him as a singer on YouTube early on. Then life happened, and he got a regular job and was taking care of his family.

I ran into Jarell in a New Orleans mall in 2015. I said, "Man, I haven't seen you in forever. What are you doing?" He told me he was just working and not really singing, so I made a mental note that when I was ready to do something, I had to call him. Not much later, I decided that I wanted to let everybody know I was home, so I started a band called Gumbeaux and we did a residency at this club called Blue Nile on Frenchmen Street in the Faubourg Marigny neighborhood. Every week, we would have a line down the block. I asked Jarell to sing in that band, and he helped me create a special vibe.

Jarell is a character. He's got a big personality and always wears these fly fedoras. He's also a jokester, clowning all the time, which is great because, like my father, I love to laugh. We're both big fans of the TV show *Martin*, with Martin Lawrence, so we're constantly throwing around *Martin* references on tour until it's time to work.

My other background singer, Tiondria Norris, is an amazing talent. I met her in 2016 when she auditioned for Solange's *A Seat at the Table* tour and I was Solange's musical director. I noticed that she auditioned for soprano—and then for tenor. She was the only woman who auditioned for tenor. That's some vocal range. Solange ended up not using her, but I made another mental note. When I started Gumbeaux, I called her and that started our relationship.

This is how dedicated Tiondria is. She found out she was pregnant while we were in Melbourne, Australia, finished that tour, then tried to do the US tour that followed, but after she had to run offstage one show in San Diego to vomit, I had her take a little break. She came back and she's a big piece of the puzzle now.

I'm talking about the people in my band because they mean everything. I pay them, but I also owe them. None of what I've done would have been possible without their talent, support, and friendship. My experiences with them changed me, too. I was becoming a leader, kind of like my dad. The band was our church, and our performances were our Sunday services.

~

In September 2008, while Kortni and I were planning our wedding, we turned all that touring into a record: *Live from LA*. We played at Temple Bar (sadly, now closed) on Wilshire Boulevard in Santa Monica, and played originals and covers for more than two hours to a packed house. We recorded the performance and chose the best tracks to reflect the energy of our shows. We played The Flamingos' "I Only Have Eyes for You," a little of Kanye's "Flashing Lights," Earth, Wind & Fire's "Can't Hide Love," and the duet "Fly Away," including a guest vocal from Anaysha Figueroa, who'd helped me cut the original. It was a great night, a great show, and a great record. A month after it came out, I was honored to play at the 2008 SoulTracks Awards in Detroit. I was having fun and I decided to take that energy back into the studio.

In 2009, I started working on what I thought might be my breakthrough solo record, *Walk Alone*. *Emotions* had been a critical success, but I was feeling stagnant, and this was my first attempt to do things differently in the studio. For the first time, I hired someone to coproduce one of my records, my mentor, Warryn Campbell. My lineup of musicians was different, because I was trying for a new sound. I still had Big Ed on drums and Jesse Bond on guitar, but now I had Calvin Parmer and Charles Chaffer on percussion, Dwayne Dugger on the sax, and James King on trumpet.

I also had my first independent-label deal. The record was a collaboration between Tehillah Music Group (a gospel label partially owned by my father), their partner IndieBlu Music, and a label I created, SOS Music. Why sign after so long being on my own? Money and distribution. I wanted a radio budget and I wanted the record to be in stores. I brought in a radio team and spent about one-third of my $75,000 budget trying to get radio airplay. This was my first time attempting that. The rest of the budget went toward making the album. It went quickly.

Walk Alone was a strong album. We did most of the recording at Dogwood Recording in Conyers, just like with *Emotions*, and mixed the record at The Hive Studios in North Hollywood, California. *Walk Alone* came out in early 2010, and I really thought it would take my career to a new level. But it didn't, and my $25,000 didn't help me make the charts at all. That hurt. I'd never had that kind of budget before, and if I hadn't wasted it on the radio promoter, I could've stretched it in all kinds of ways: social media, YouTube, and more.

It was discouraging, especially because I was finally realizing something: *I wanted a hit.* What I couldn't have known at the time was that I was about to become part of one of the greatest hit-making machines in popular music.

Chapter Eleven

On My Way

Mack Maine, president of Young Money Entertainment, was a year ahead of me at St. Augustine High School. We knew each other, but we weren't really close. But later, I learned that Mack is a protector. He wants to see everybody win. That's what he's always been about. He was a rapper himself, but the thing he loves the most is putting people in positions to win. I've always loved that about him.

I bring up Mack because we were driving around Miami together in early 2010 when a Maroon 5 song came on the radio. Mack said, "Man, Maroon 5 is my favorite band." It was a throwaway comment I didn't even think about at the time. Then I said, "You know they just came out with a new song?" That was "Misery," and we found it on the radio. It was great.

For years, I had admired Maroon's melodies, their blend of pop, funk, rock, and "blue-eyed soul," and their ability to evolve with the times while still sounding distinctive. I was a fan. So it was fateful when, a couple of weeks later, I got a call from my friend Adam Blackstone, who was coming in as Maroon's musical director.

Maroon had just finished recording its album *Hands All Over* in Switzerland, and they wanted to bring in a new keyboard player and singer to help them with the tour for that record. They had reached out to Questlove of The Roots, but The Roots had just signed to be the house band for *Late Night with Jimmy Fallon*, so Questlove wasn't available. Questlove recommended that Maroon reach out to Adam, and when Adam sat down with the guys, they asked him if he knew a keyboard player who could sing. Adam recommended me, and then called me to see if I was interested.

You might be surprised to find that I was. I was a little burned out from the grind of recording, touring, and not getting anywhere. I was three shows from the end of the *Walk Alone* tour, and I had no idea what I was going to do after that tour ended. So when Adam said, "Hey, man, do you like Maroon 5?" I was listening.

Adam knew I didn't want to be a gigging musician, so he didn't call me about regular gigs. But Maroon 5 was different, because I wouldn't be just another keyboard player in the background. I would be *in* the band, sort of, at least temporarily. I said, "Yeah, I've always liked Maroon 5," which was true, and Adam said he'd pass my name along to the guys.

Adam called back and told me that the band wanted to hold auditions. They wanted to make sure whoever they brought into the band could not only play but also had good chemistry with the guys. But I had never auditioned in my life. Either I was in charge of the recording session or gig, the people involved already knew who I was, or I got the job through a personal contact.

The guys from Maroon had never held an audition, either. Most of them had been playing together since eighth grade, so this would be the first time they had ever brought in anyone from outside. There was a guy named Tommy King who played on a college tour right before I came along, but he didn't audition; he just helped out. But I had nothing to lose, so I agreed to the audition and flew to Los Angeles.

I was the first person to audition. I don't know if that made it easier or harder, but I just decided I would go in and be my normal self. I didn't know how to prepare, so I didn't. Ignorance is bliss. They had asked me to learn their song "Sunday Morning," so I worked on it at my parents' house before I left. It's a simple song, so when I got to LA, I was able to play it with the band, and as soon as we started playing, it was like we'd been playing together for years. We all just vibed with each other. After we'd finished, they asked me what other songs of theirs I knew, and I knew a bunch of them. I sincerely was a Maroon fan long before that audition. So we played "This Love" and some other tunes I knew by ear, and we had the same easy chemistry.

We were having such a good time that the audition went on longer than it was supposed to, but they had a guy scheduled after me so we eventually shook hands and I left. But as soon as I got back to my hotel, I got a call. They had canceled the second day of auditions. Did I want to be in Maroon 5?

Yes.

~

The guys in Maroon are like family to me now. Jesse Carmichael is the reason I'm in the band, and because we're both keyboard players, we have that connection. So that's kind of where we meet each other. He was my number one cheerleader when I auditioned, because I don't think everybody was bought in right away.

Adam Levine is probably who I have the most in common with. Our tastes in clothes and sneakers are the closest, and we're the only ones who play basketball, so we'll hoop together. When we do arena tours, we'll play ball at the NBA gyms. We've had NBA players come out to shoot with us, which is very cool. Years ago, when he saw me going back to my solo career, Adam said something that really touched me. "If you get as big as us, and you have to co-headline," he said, "we're going to do that." He's a really loyal person.

I have a whole different dynamic with guitarist and backup singer James Valentine. James and I probably have the deepest conversations. Not that Adam's not a deep thinker, but we mostly talk about stuff like clothes or music. James and I have deeper conversations about things like politics or new technology. We've even talked about the dynamics of the band and what we're doing in the future. James is a hardcore tennis player, but he's fully into pickleball right now. He played in Africa. He played in France. It doesn't matter what country or city, he finds pickleball.

Matt Flynn, the drummer, and I are the jokesters of the band. That's who I clown with the most. We're always coming up with bits, but a lot of them are inappropriate. We've even talked about having our own podcast where we could play good cop, bad cop. Sam Farrar is the only member who came after me, but he was in a big band, Phantom Planet, before joining Maroon. He's an amazing producer and songwriter, and Sam and I make the most music outside of the band. He'll say, "I'm trying to do double duty like you, but I can't make this date. What should I do?" He's seen me juggle for years.

I've got a million Maroon stories, but one of the most memorable was when we did a twenty-four-hour songwriting challenge with Coca-Cola. We had to write and record a new song in twenty-four hours while people were watching live online and sending in ideas via live stream. That was the only time I wrote a song for Maroon. Adam was so tired that he fell asleep and I wrote the bridge of this tune called, "Is Anybody Out There?"

We were trapped in that studio with the whole world watching. It was a kind of torture. Nobody could pick their nose or tell an off-color joke, and once we got to hour nineteen, we were all dead. So we had to start napping in shifts.

～

I played my first show for Maroon in New York on July 27, 2010. Later, when the band went on tour for *Hands All Over* in 2011, I was a touring member, but I wasn't visible, and I wasn't writing songs for the band. Ironically, I had finally achieved what I had wanted in those years when I was too shy to be a frontman: I was the guy sitting behind the keyboards, playing and singing backing vocals, the guy nobody knew. My life and career really are a collection of ironies.

Touring for *Hands All Over* was a completely new experience for me. We played our first show on February 16, 2011, in Bristol, England, and finished on July 21, 2012, in Nevada, playing a total of sixty-one shows in places like Ireland, Germany, Turkey, Dubai, Thailand, Australia, Japan, the Philippines, and Brazil. It was incredible. I was experiencing touring with a big-time pop act, which meant first-rate hotels, spacious tour buses, and first-class flights. No more Mom's church bus!

In March 2012, Jesse announced that he was going to take a sabbatical from the band for a while, and I agreed to fill in for him until he came back. I didn't know that I was being prepared for something bigger, but I guess I was. After two years of me being the invisible man in the band, I started popping up in publicity photos and on CD cases. Hey, all of a sudden there was a Black dude in Maroon 5!

When Jesse rejoined the band in August of that year, the guys asked me to stay as a permanent member. Now we were a six-man lineup. On the next record, *Overexposed*, I started getting credited. That was the first album that I was a part of, and it was the album where the band went from popular to globally gigantic.

The call from Maroon had come at a critical point in my life. I was happily married to Kortni, but that was the only part of my life where I was really happy. After *Walk Alone*, I felt stagnant. I was frustrated with my career because I had been doing the same thing over and over. I would write new songs, record a new album, go on tour, pack the same clubs, and put on some terrific shows, but at the end of the day I wasn't growing commercially or artistically. I needed to make music a different way for a while, and Maroon came along at the perfect time.

I got more than I'd bargained for from the experience. I had joined the band at a pivotal moment in their trajectory as well. In 2011, Maroon was popular but hadn't made the final leap to worldwide superstardom. The unspoken question within the band was, *Are we going to stay where we are, or are we going to go to the moon?* Then came "Moves Like Jagger," which changed everything. Adam joined *The Voice*, and Maroon went to the moon.

By 2012, Maroon was bigger than ever. When I joined in 2010, the band was playing for five thousand people. After "Jagger" hit number one on the *Billboard* charts in June 2011, things went nuts. On the *Overexposed* tour, we sold out sports stadiums and arenas with capacities of twenty thousand people or more. It was new for everybody. Before I came along, Maroon had released successful records, gone on successful tours, and charted a bunch of hits. But none of us had experienced anything like this.

For me, Maroon was part of a deliberate decision to be big and be pop, at least part of the time. But I still wanted to grow my career as a soul musician, because I had more that I wanted to say. So, starting in 2012, I had two careers.

~

One common denominator in the good things that have happened to me is that I've been willing to say "yes" when an opportunity came along, even if that opportunity wasn't what I had in mind. I said yes to Erykah Badu about going on tour. I said yes to becoming a father figure for Jakai. I said yes to Maroon. None of these opportunities was part of my plan at the time. I said yes because I think being open to opportunities—especially the unexpected ones—is a great way to break out of a rut and grow in ways you didn't even know you needed.

The other thing I've learned is that it's important to be a good person and a professional. I've built a reputation not only as a good musician and a professional, but as a good dude. Without that reputation, I never would have gotten that call from Adam Black-stone, and I wouldn't be in Maroon. It makes you think.

In August 2012, Maroon started the *Overexposed* tour, which, apart from a four-month break at the end of 2012, continued until January 2014. This was the big time. What could have been more perfect? I was enjoying massive mainstream success, traveling and playing in front of enormous crowds, and doing it all with a group of guys who quickly became like brothers to me.

The other big change that came as a result of being in Maroon was where I called home. Other than my brief stay in the Bronx after Katrina, I had made Atlanta my home since 1999. That's where my family of musicians was located. That's where I pro-duced. But being a member of Maroon had changed the math for me. Paying the bills wasn't an issue anymore, but the fact that the guys kept flying me out to Los Angeles for rehearsals was.

By now, I was constantly traveling across the country to work with the band. Before long, it became clear that this wasn't sus-tainable. Not only was all that travel exhausting for me and hard on my family, but I felt like the guys would really rather have me in LA full-time. Once, Adam said, "Man, I would love it if you were in LA." But otherwise they never said a word about it. Still, I felt bad. I had been burned out before Maroon, and they wel-comed me with open arms. They had put their faith in me, and I wanted to show them that I was one hundred percent committed. So, about seven months after P3 was born, we made the move to Los Angeles.

To be exact, we moved to the city of Burbank, which Johnny Carson made famous on the old *Tonight Show*. If you know LA, you might be saying, *Burbank, PJ? Seriously? Not Beverly Hills, Santa Monica, or West Hollywood?* Those are some of the glamorous parts of the city, but I loved Burbank. It was unpretentious, it was familiar to me from my work as a producer and songwriter, and it was central to everything I needed, including Fever Studios in North Hollywood, which was owned by Warryn Campbell.

Just like that, Kortni and I and our two kids were living in a two-bedroom apartment in Burbank, and it was great. It was all new. Los Angeles, of course, is nothing like Atlanta. The vibe was new, the weather was completely different, and the artistic scene was all about movies and television. I could afford to take it all in, because I was in the city for something that was very stable. And as soon as I had settled in, Maroon started calling rehearsals out of the blue: *Let's do this, let's run that.*

Rehearsal with Maroon is a well-oiled machine. It usually happens in a rehearsal studio, the same one I auditioned in. A crew usually gets there sometime before us, and my keyboard tech has my keyboard set up, making sure all the sounds I need are already loaded. When the band files in, most of the time we use a skeleton set that Adam has worked on as a starting point. Sometimes we'll gather around the whiteboard, but Jesse's usually the one who does the writing, although James has the best handwriting.

Before we play, we start to build a set. Everybody has opinions, but it's really democratic. It's just ideas. What could be cool? What would be a good transition? Do we need to play this song? Do we need to play that song? Then we just start grooving on something. It could be an actual song. It could be a cover song. Sometimes it's just a groove that we fall into to get loose.

I hate long rehearsals, and one thing I love about Maroon is that our rehearsals are tight. If we're working with the older stuff, we might transition to one of the newer songs, or we could decide the song needs a new ending. Sometimes, we'll go back to the old songs, the ones we've played a million times, just to make sure we still know how to play them. But we never go on longer than we have to.

The best thing is, I get to be with some of my closest friends at work. We're eating, taking lunch breaks, talking about whatever's happened that day, and making a lot of jokes. When it's time to work and do the music, we're all business. Otherwise, there's a lot of laughing.

A few months after relocating, we moved from our apartment into a house and I rented studio space nearby. A few months after that, Peyton was born, "Moves Like Jagger" took Maroon into the stratosphere, and it was on. I've always felt kind of rootless, and I enjoy moving into new territory and trying something different. I loved the adventure of being in LA. It was an exciting time. I had high hopes that this would be when my career started following the trajectory I had always imagined it would.

~

I've been with Maroon for fourteen years now, and as far as I'm concerned, I'll be part of Maroon until we're all too old to do this anymore. Those guys are my brothers. Between the dream of being part of such a popular group, and the incredible relationships I've built with the guys, it's important to me that my membership in Maroon stands on its own. It's not something I'm using as a stepping-stone for my career as a soul artist.

Yes, as I get busier, it's challenging to squeeze everything in. Sometimes the guys and I have to talk about the shows I can't do. When I went on a month-long tour of Africa in 2023, we had to manage the logistics of that. But we figure stuff like that out together. They've seen all the solo success I've had and done nothing but support me. I owe those guys so much.

At the same time, I'm super careful to keep life with "the Five" separate from my life as a solo artist. I don't get into the business of Maroon. I play on the albums. I'm the keyboard player in the center of the stage and I do my thing. My solo career is so much work that it's a relief when I'm with Maroon, because I don't have to be in control. That frees me to just be a keyboard player, singer, and performer. If I write a song one day that everybody in the band likes and wants to record, cool. But that's not my role. I just have a good time. That's a hard career to beat.

Chapter Twelve

Claustrophobic

There's an old saying that goes, "Be careful what you wish for, because you might get it." But now I had everything I had wished for, and I was very happy. For years, I had wanted to be just the guy who played keyboard and sang while someone else took the role of frontman and stood in the spotlight. Now, amazingly, I could be that guy in the background while one of the greatest front men in the business, Adam Levine, sang and worked the audience. Even better, I got to do this for a band that sells more records than practically any other act on earth.

At the same time, I had the freedom to pursue my solo projects with the increased visibility that came with being a member of Maroon. Remind me again why I should be careful what I wish for?

Around the same time Maroon was happening, something else big was going down in my career, something I thought was another dream come true. For a while, it looked like it was. But what it did was confirm everything about what I didn't want from my career. Maybe the saying should be, "Be careful what you wish for, because it might change who you think you are."

～

Mack Maine and I had a mutual friend in New Orleans: Ezra Landry, who grew up in New Orleans in the same neighborhood as Mack. Ezra knew everybody and connected everybody, and he would come to the church to hear me play and sing. He kept me on Mack's radar.

By 2010, I was performing with Maroon and I was cool with being an independent solo artist. I was good at it. I could bring together people to make amazing music and put together a tour that would draw. Because of my marketing background, I knew to pay attention to the presentation—CD art, posters, flyers. When you're independent, everything has to look high-quality and professional. My brand always looked on par with the big labels.

I had redefined what the music industry looked like for me. My success wasn't based on having hits. I was surviving and touring the way I wanted to and making music the way I wanted to without having to compromise. But what I didn't tell anyone was that I was tired. Tired of touring and spending money and promoting my records only to get nowhere.

All artists doubt themselves, and I was starting to wonder, "Am I not who I think I am?" Some part of me wanted a little validation that I was making good music. I knew my fans loved me, but I really wanted my music to reach more people. That meant signing with a major label.

As I've said, from time to time I would travel with my dad when he preached, and when he went to Miami in 2010, I went with him and hung out with Mack Maine. We talked about Maroon and about the possibility of me signing with Young Money Entertainment. The label was founded in 2005 by Lil Wayne as an imprint of Cash Money Records. To date, they've had fifteen records that have gone to number one. Young Money was also part of Universal Music Group and one of the most important players in rap and hip-hop.

Mack and his people loved *Walk Alone*, and we had started talking about me signing with Young Money even before I got the call from Maroon. After I became part of Maroon, the talks got even heavier. I would be more visible as part of one of the most popular bands in the country, and I could take my own music in a fresh new direction. It was incredibly exciting.

I had wanted to be with a major label for years, but I had assumed it would never happen. Wait, what about being a proud, fiercely independent artist? Well, I was still proud of what I had done, but I thought I had exhausted everything I could do as an indie. I was bored and frustrated, and I needed to figure things out. But more importantly, my *reason* for wanting to be with a major had changed.

When I was younger, I thought getting signed was the only way I could record, release records, and play live. I didn't know the independent path yet. By 2010, I knew that if I wanted to, I could spend the rest of my life doing things my way, but I didn't want to do that anymore. Signing with a major would give me access to artists and resources I'd never had access to before, which would let me try things I had never tried before.

At the time, Young Money was the biggest, hottest label in the world with the biggest names in the business: Lil Wayne, Nicki Minaj, Drake, Tyga. When word got out that I might sign with them, friends started calling me hoping I could score them some YMCMB merch. I was thinking, *I'm in Maroon, and I can sign with the hottest label in the country and be their only R&B singer!* It made sense, even though it was a strange match. Simply put, it was a once-in-a-lifetime opportunity that was too good to pass up.

The signing process with Young Money took about a year, with attorneys going back and forth, but finally, in December 2011, I signed with Young Money Entertainment and Mack's production company, Soothe Your Soul Entertainment. I can remember standing in our kitchen in Burbank holding the Young Money contract in my hands. I can smell the ink. It had taken forever to negotiate the points of the deal, but I couldn't believe that I was finally getting a major label deal with the hottest label in the business. Holding the pen in my hand, I knew once I had signed, things would never be the same.

I put the papers on the kitchen table and signed them. After the holidays, Mack put out a press statement that said:

I signed PJ because his music does not just soothe your ears, it soothes your soul. His music truly impacts your emotions and gets into your mind. We have known PJ is a special artist for many years and now with Young Money Entertainment being able to share his music at large, the whole world will get to know.

I started working on my first record, an EP called *Following My First Mind*, which came out on March 27, 2012.

~

Following My First Mind was a seven-track EP, a warm-up project that let me test out how much artistic freedom Young Money/ Cash Money would give me. I blended hard beats with the string arrangements I'd always used on my records, and I liked that I would be introducing Young Money's fans to a soul sound. "Following my first mind" is a personal mantra that refers to the need for creative people to trust our instincts.

After *Following My First Mind* dropped, I got to work on my major label debut, *New Orleans*. I wanted to make a tribute to my hometown, where I had fallen in love with music before I had to think about things like marketing, radio airplay, and paying for tour buses. New Orleans was about making music, pure and simple.

Of course, working with a major label was a little different. I didn't realize how different. I had always made records my way because I was paying for them. For example, I was used to booking a studio, so imagine how surprised I was when someone from Young Money said, "Just tell us where you want to record and we'll book it and pay for it." Whoa. This was a whole new world.

Even my "Welcome to the Label" party in New York caught me by surprise. I didn't know that the label had a car service for me, so I caught a ride with Brian. When I rolled up to the Canal Room, a classic New York live music venue, I saw that this party was a big deal. Busta Rhymes was there. Lil Wayne was there. When I told them I'd hitched a ride with my bass player, they were shocked. Katrina from Universal said, "Wait, you didn't take your car?" I honestly didn't know I *had* a car. I was too independent for my own good. That was part of my learning curve.

Recording required some adjustments, too. At first, I was fine with calling the label when I was ready to go into the studio. But I liked moving when I was ready, and calling slowed me down. Then it came time to record, and I got to work at Paramount Studios in Los Angeles—the historic studios where artists like Michael Jackson, Jimi Hendrix, Bruno Mars, and Kendrick Lamar have made records—and I figured I would adjust. Making the record was similar to my process, except that I wasn't paying for it and I got to use the resources I wanted to use. I had access to Busta Rhymes! I was also able to have different conversations because I was part of a winning team.

Another thing I liked about Young Money was that they didn't bother me. Nobody ever said, "You've got to make this. We got to have Lil Wayne on this song." They didn't even hear my album until it was complete. Any pressure came from me feeling like I had to deliver. I was on a major label, so I had to step up in a different way. Artists had been signing with Young Money for years but they never seemed to release anything apart from Drake, Lil Wayne, Nicki Minaj, and Tyga. There were a lot of artists who had been signed for a long time but hadn't had their releases. I didn't want to be one of them.

When it came to musical choices, my attitude was, *If I'm going to do this, let's aim high.* My biggest concern was repeating myself. I wanted to keep things fresh and original. I started to think about collaborators. I had already gotten some huge names to contribute to *Following My First Mind.* Lil Wayne had appeared on a song called "Lover," while Adam Levine did a fantastic duet with me on "Heavy," and Busta Rhymes had appeared on a track called "Never Get Over You." But *New Orleans* would be my coming-out party, so I decided to aim even higher. Who do you think I went after?

Right. Stevie Wonder himself.

~

Sometimes, I can hardly believe that today, Stevie and I are friends and collaborators. We've worked on songs together. I've got his personal cell number and can call him anytime. But whenever I'm around him, I'm still that fourteen-year-old kid standing there in awe. After all, he was my muse. Kirk Franklin, the great gospel musician, introduced me to him backstage at a show once, but that was just a quick "I love you, I'm such a fan" meet and greet. Nothing Stevie would have remembered.

When I signed my deal with Young Money, I thought, *I finally have a real budget; I'm going after Stevie Wonder.* I wrote a song, "Only One," that felt like a Stevie song, because he was always in my head. But I had no way to get it to him. The only person I knew who knew him was his drummer, Teddy Campbell. I hit Teddy up and he told me the best way to get the song to Stevie was to give it to his stylist, April, who just happened to be from New Orleans and was a fan of mine. I gave her a copy of the song on CD and kept my fingers crossed. I wasn't hopeful, because Stevie didn't need to do anything for me. He was already a superstar, so the only way he would even consider collaborating with me was if he really liked the song.

A few weeks later, I heard from April. I was on tour with Maroon and she sent me a video. I opened it on my phone and there was Stevie, messing around at the piano with "Only One," playing the progressions and singing my lyrics. *Oh my God.* I had an out-of-body experience. A few months later, when I was recording *New Orleans*, what I'd been dreaming of happened: Stevie Wonder played harmonica on "Only One," which became my second single and first solo Grammy nomination. The only reason I didn't cry when I listened to him playing was that I was in shock.

Still, it wasn't like Stevie and I were hanging on the regular. In 2014, I was on a flight and standing in line for the lavatory when I felt a figure behind me. You usually see Stevie sitting at the piano or keyboard, so it's easy to forget he's six feet tall. I'm only five-six, so when I turned, Stevie was looming over me, waiting for the bathroom like a regular person. I took a deep breath and said, "Yo, Stevie, it's PJ Morton. You just did my song, 'Only One.'" He smiled that big smile and said, "Oh, man, you can sing." That's all I remember, because my mind went blank when he said that. I thanked him for being on the record and then let him go ahead of me into the bathroom.

The next time we connected was at JazzFest in New Orleans in 2017. Stevie always has a keyboard backstage anywhere he performs, so when he woke up from a nap, he and Corinne Bailey Rae, an English singer-songwriter, started working on a song together on the piano. Mike Phillips, Stevie's saxophone player, knew I loved Stevie and had been pushing for us to hang out. He said to me, "I'm going to make sure you're around. I know he's gonna love you." So there I was, backstage, just listening.

Then Stevie and Corinne started singing, and without thinking, I started singing a second harmony. (Somewhere, I have video of the three of us singing.) When he heard my voice, Stevie stopped, cocked his head, and said, "Who's that?" I said, "Stevie, It's PJ Morton." Because he's blind, Stevie touches a lot, so he reached out, took my arm, and said, "Yeah. Yeah. Hey, man. All right." Then he asked me, "What song do you want to do with me today?"

I didn't know what to say. Even though my fandom for Stevie is way beyond my fandom for anyone else, that doesn't mean I know every word of every song. It's deeper and more spiritual than that for me. Finally, I said, "Just whatever, man. I don't really know lyrics." Whatever the song was, I'd have to look at the words.

Next thing I knew, I was standing with Stevie for the pre-show prayer, and we went on together and ended up doing "Living for the City." I had connected with my idol and performed with him, and it was all I could have ever hoped for. But I thought it couldn't possibly get better than that.

I was wrong.

Since 1979, Stevie has owned an R&B radio station in Los Angeles, KJLH FM, and he's more involved in it than people realize. In fact, he's listening all the time. When my breakout album, *Gumbo*, came out later in 2017, it included the song "First Began." Apparently Stevie heard the song and loved it, so when KJLH staged its annual music festival in Inglewood, I received an invitation to come to the festival and talk shop with Stevie.

It was just me and him, hanging in his trailer, talking about music. That's when he told me that "First Began" was his favorite song from *Gumbo*. He said, "Me and my wife cried to that song. Man, I wish I wrote that." That was the greatest compliment I've ever gotten in my life. After he said it, I was thinking, *I don't have to write anything else, ever.* Maybe he was just being nice, but I didn't care.

Later in the day Stevie told me, "I want to work on some stuff," and that's when we became collaborators. I got his phone number. That was the first time I ever felt comfortable with him, like we could be friends, even peers. Somewhere, there's video from that day of me on stage doing "First Began," and you can see Stevie swaying and clapping, a huge grin on his face. That was a dream day for me.

But while I had Stevie's number, I was nervous about using it. Stevie himself made it easier. He called me to ask me to sing on one of his new songs, a duet called "Where Did All Your Happy Go?," and produced my vocals (another dream come true). From time to time, he would leave me encouraging voice mails like, "Don't stop" and "You're needed." Finally, when I wrote "Be Like Water" for *Watch the Sun*, I saw the perfect opportunity to ask him to collaborate.

I sent him an early version of the song, and later I got a voice mail from him saying, "I love it. I love it," while he played and sang some of "Be Like Water." It started to feel like we were buddies. I'll never get completely comfortable with him, because it's still Stevie. But today, it feels like there's mutual respect.

I'm forever grateful. Stevie's my hero. They say, "Never meet your heroes," but I met mine and he was even greater than I thought he could be. He's the reason I'm doing what I do. He's the reason I say things the way I say them, play the way I do, and even write progressions like I do. It all starts with Stevie.

~

Stevie playing harmonica on "Only One" was a dream come true for me, the kid who devoured every one of his CDs back in the 1990s. I also got the band back together. I got Warryn Campbell to coproduce some stuff with me; brought in Jesse Bond, Brian, and Big Ed on guitar, bass, and drums; and got James Valentine from Maroon to lend a hand on guitar. I even had Stephanie Matthews, the violinist who had been kicked out of the Erykah Badu concert, lead a big string section. You'll notice that even though I was excited about having access to bigger names, I came home to the people who had become family.

Still, I took advantage of Young Money clout where I could. I had dreamed about having the great Manny Marroquin mix a song for me. Manny's a legendary engineer who's mixed the likes of Rihanna, Kanye West, Katy Perry, Ed Sheeran, Taylor Swift, Post Malone, and more. His work made me pay attention to what mixing was. I listened to his records and said, "Why does this sound so good?" But I could never have gotten to Manny without a major label. When I signed my deal, I said, "I want Manny to mix this." It was one of my first requests, and when I made the record, Manny was one of my engineers.

In my mind, *New Orleans* was about to be the biggest thing ever.

~

The record dropped on May 14, 2013, from Young Money, Cash Money, and Republic Records. To help promote it, I did something I hadn't done in three years: I asked Maroon for a favor. Would they be cool with me opening for Maroon as PJ Morton, and then playing with the band? The guys all knew I had signed with a major label, and they were happy for me. They also knew I needed to push the record, so they said yes. That's why on the *Overexposed* tour, there was a run of shows where "PJ Morton" is listed as the opening act, and then later on, there I was again, playing keyboard on "Payphone" and "Moves Like Jagger."

It didn't matter. The record got great reviews, but didn't catch any heat. *New Orleans* topped out at #194 on the *Billboard 200*.

The first single, "Lover" with Lil Wayne, went nowhere. Neither did "Only One," the song featuring Stevie Wonder. This was incredibly frustrating to me, and it got me second-guessing myself about signing. Why hadn't I stuck to my guns and stayed independent? *New Orleans* was an eye-opener, because it showed me that even a player like Young Money can't just push a button and make something a hit. If they couldn't get me a hit with their resources and reputation, how were they any different from me?

Don't get me wrong. I loved working with Mack and the artists I had collaborated with, and getting a close-up look at the industry. Young Money had let me make the record I wanted to make without interference. I had a budget to do all the things I had ever wanted. I had billboards all over New Orleans and Atlanta, and wrapped buses on the streets of Los Angeles. It was able to get my music out to more people.

In December 2013, I even got my first Grammy nomination as a solo artist: Best R&B Song for "Only One." Back then, it was difficult to get nominated as an independent, so I knew my nomination had been made possible by the increased visibility that came from being on a major label. I was proud of *New Orleans* and grateful to Young Money. But I had made the deal to get hits, and it hadn't happened. I wasn't sure where that left me.

The trouble was, Young Money didn't know what to do with me. The business model for rap and hip-hop is different from that of soul and R&B. Rappers release mixtapes. They'll rap over someone else's beat or someone else's song and release it for free. In soul, you make the record then go on the road and play it. We were speaking different languages. The independent world moves fast. I needed to release things without asking anyone's permission, but the majors don't work that way. I had to wait for dates and email responses before I could make a move. If there was something I needed to move quickly on, a Universal rep might tell me, "Taylor Swift is coming out, you've got to wait." It drove me crazy.

~

Something else happened in 2013 that made me question my past choices and ended up determining the course of my future: Maroon was booked to headline the New Orleans Jazz & Heritage Festival. I introduced the guys to the city where I was born.

I had grown up going to JazzFest. I played it as a junior in high school with the St. Augustine jazz band, with Freestyle Nation, and as a solo artist. But I had never headlined it. On a cool, damp day, we shared the stage with Willie Nelson and reggae legend Jimmy Cliff. It was amazing.

That time in New Orleans also opened my eyes. To me, the city was home, and when I went home, I normally took a break, hung out with friends, and chilled. I didn't sightsee. Why would I? But this trip was different. I didn't see my family or go to my normal spots, because the band had stuff to do. Meanwhile, the guys from Maroon were tripping over New Orleans—the houses, the architecture, the food, the street life, everything. The city was so familiar to me that I normally shrugged at all the things that got visitors so excited. But on that visit, I saw the city through my friends' eyes.

Looking at it from the perspective of my bandmates, New Orleans blew my mind. One of them pointed at a block in the Garden District and shouted, "I love these houses!" and I shouted back, "Yeah, me too!" It was like I was seeing my city for the first time and noticing things I had never noticed before. That planted a seed. When I left New Orleans to go to Atlanta, I thought I would never move back. I wasn't a jazz musician. I didn't want to be in my father's shadow. It wasn't my place anymore. That trip with Maroon was the first time I ever thought, *Yeah, I could live here.*

By the end of that year, I had started to think about doing another album with Young Money, but I didn't know if that was the right thing for me. I wanted the best of both worlds: to operate as an independent within a major system, using all my experience and my marketing skills. But the label couldn't give me that. There were too many checks and balances.

I also had writer's block at the time, which comes out of nowhere for me. Usually, writer's block means I need to stop trying and just be present for a while, so I decided to set up meetings at other big labels. If I found one I liked and decided to ask for my release from Young Money, I would have options.

I also hoped these meetings would help me be present and jolt me out of my writer's block, but they were just depressing and infuriating. Nobody seemed to get me, or to even want to get me. The worst meeting was one I took at the suggestion of a close friend, a successful songwriter I'd met after coming to California. There was another person in the meeting who worked with my friend, but I didn't really know him.

We sat down in a conference room at the label's offices, the meeting started, and this second guy started trashing my music! He was having conversations about me, without me being involved, while I was sitting two chairs away. The executives asked him about my music and he said, "I think it's a little dated. I think it could be updated." He went on giving notes about my music, while I had no idea what was happening. Then one of the guys from the label said, "Have you thought about having him work with DJ Mustard?"

DJ Mustard was the hottest hip-hop producer around at the time—and no disrespect to him because I'm a fan of his music—but he produces a lot of modern club hip-hop and R&B, which is nothing like the soul music I was making. Obviously, the guy talking about my music didn't care what it sounded like. He was making the suggestion based only on the possibility of having hits.

In fact, nobody in the meeting knew anything about me or my music. After a while, the people in the meeting all started to sound like the teacher in the Charlie Brown cartoons: "Wah wah wah, wah wah wah…" I felt like I was shrinking or had been down-loaded into the Matrix. It was humiliating. I was a commodity, and the sooner I accepted that, the better, because then I would understand how the game worked. But it was a game I didn't want to play. I don't remember how the meeting ended, but before I got out of there, I was thinking, *I've got to leave LA.*

I didn't leave right then. I didn't say anything to Kortni. I even went to more label meetings that were almost as bad. The only good part was that I broke my writer's block. I wrote a new song, "Claustrophobic." It was my clap-back at the small-minded executives who told me they loved everything about my music, except my music.

～

The 2014 Grammys were held on January 26, 2014, at Staples Center in Los Angeles, and I was in my seat, just excited to be a nominee. Best R&B Song is awarded to songwriters, and "Only

One" was up against some great songs: "Pusher Love Girl," "Best of Me," "Love and War," and "Without Me."

It was a special day. The Grammys have always been synonymous with my heroes, like Quincy Jones, Michael Jackson, and Stevie, the legends who made me want to be a musician. Being nominated was important. The Grammys are awarded based on the votes of your peers, and anyone who tells you that recognition from your peers doesn't feel good is lying. It was extra special because my dad was nominated, too, for his album *Best Days Yet*. We were the first father and son nominated in the same year since Bob and Jakob Dylan in 1998.

To this point, I'd been nominated only as part of group projects: the India.Arie record in 2002 (a win) and Maroon nominations in 2013 for *Overexposed* and "Payphone" (both losses). When the 2014 award was announced that night, "Pusher Love Girl" took it home. I was a little disappointed, but I had known it would be an uphill battle to win. I figured I would have lots of other chances.

My family and I were still in LA. Maroon was working hard on a new album, which would become *V* and spin off the single "Sugar." But I was at a crossroads with my solo career. Young Money had granted my request and released me from my contract, so I was a free agent, but I'd lost my interest in signing with a label. I loved playing live, but I also wanted to be back in the studio. I'm a workaholic, remember? Then an idea I'd been messing with came back to me: bring together my band in a studio, but bring in the energy of a live audience. I ended up renting Jim Henson Studios in Los Angeles, where they recorded "We Are the World" back in 1985, and brought in my band, a stage, and an audience.

We brought cameras into the studio so people on Periscope could watch us record live. I reunited with my old band, including Big Ed, and we had a great time playing through favorites from earlier records, including "Mountains and Molehills" and "Lover." I did a duet with gospel/soul artist Mali Music on "Heavy," and Tweet sang with me on "Love You More" from *Walk Alone*. We also did covers of "Try a Little Tenderness" and "Thank You for Being a Friend." We drew on Chicago blues, Motown, and gospel, and the audience energy was sky-high.

The result became *Live Show Killer with PJ Morton & The Crusade*, released in July 2015. But as soon as the music met the real world, it disappeared. We toured, and fans enjoyed the shows, but sales were flat, and so was I. I was sick of working so hard to make independent music nobody cared about. I felt lost and far from my roots. My writer's block was back, too. Songwriting usually comes easily for me. My home and studio are stacked with notebooks filled with handwritten song titles and musical ideas. But I had nothing. I needed a break—from the industry, from LA, maybe even from music.

At least one good thing came out of 2015, though: Wade Jordan. I met Wade back when he worked for Verity Records, the label DeWayne Woods was on when he recorded my song "Let Go" in 2006. Later on, Wade managed DeWayne, and I worked with him as I collaborated with DeWayne numerous times over the years. One day in 2015, Wade called me out of the blue and suggested the possibility of him managing me. I was looking at other managers at the time and told him I wasn't sure, but regardless, he got to work! He told me, "I don't need the title of manager," and he didn't. That's just who Wade is. He's all about results and we connect on that. It's been almost ten years now and we've never had a contract.

But as 2015 ended, Wade was the only positive development in my career. After *New Orleans*, my humiliating record label meetings, the Grammy loss, my writer's block, and making *Live Show Killer* only to watch it do nothing commercially, I felt cynical and burned out. I was ready to get out of LA. I wanted to move back to New Orleans. I wanted to go home.

A few days later I told Kortni, "I'm done." But she's my best friend. She already knew. She'd seen the little disappointments piling up. When Maroon was nominated in 2015 for Best Pop Duo/Group Performance for "Sugar" and we were getting ready to go to the Grammy ceremony, she said, "Why do we still go to these things?" She was surprised when I told her about New Orleans, because she had just started to get settled in LA. But she trusts my crazy brain and my crazy decisions. That's why she's crisscrossed the states with me a few times.

The lease was up on our LA house, so we didn't think too much. We hired somebody to help pack up the house, and then I had to go out on tour with Maroon. I was nervous about telling the guys that I was going to move, because they had been my reason for moving to Los Angeles in the first place. But they were incredible. They agreed that I didn't need to be in LA to be an important part of the band. We'd see each other at gigs, and I would still fly out to rehearse and record. Things were so locked in for Maroon that I knew what was happening two years ahead of time. Planning would be easy.

With Maroon's blessing, when our tour ended in February 2016, I followed my family to where it all started. I just didn't know what I was going to do when I got there.

Chapter Thirteen

Home Again

Who wants to buy some sneakers?

That's what I was thinking when Kortni and I settled in New Orleans. Music wasn't on my mind. I had decided to open a sneaker store. I'm a "sneakerhead." I love shoes and can talk about them all day long. New Orleans didn't have a high-end sneaker store for sneaker fanatics like me, so I figured I would do my entrepreneurial thing and come back to music in the future. Until that happened, I would get plenty of performance time with Maroon.

When my mom and dad found out we were bringing their grandchildren back to New Orleans, they celebrated. A lot of my friends, on the other hand, were confused. I got a lot of, "Why are you moving back here?" I understood. I hadn't lived there since 1999. I would come back and do shows, but I would never stay long. I didn't really have a clear idea myself, honestly. New Orleans was a safe place to land. I needed to reset and reconnect. That was it.

As I settled in, I started to realize how lucky I'd been to be born in New Orleans. I didn't appreciate that when I was growing up, because it was my father's town. He cast a big shadow. When people looked at me, they saw a younger version of him. They didn't see me. They didn't understand my music, and I was looked down upon because I didn't read music.

But coming back—wow. I found myself thinking, *This city gave me so much.* I didn't realize how unique it was until I'd been everywhere else in the world with Maroon. There is no place like it. When I think of New Orleans, what comes to mind is *integrity*. Not food, not tourism. There's such integrity here when it comes to music. You can play around with everything else, but if you're going to do music in New Orleans, you'd better treat it as a serious thing. Music is our survival. It's our lifeline. You don't pick up an instrument in New Orleans unless you're ready to play. I joke a lot and I'm lighthearted, but not about this. There's an old quote that goes, "Some people believe football is a matter of life and death. I can assure you it is much more important than that." That's music to New Orleans.

An experience that really drove that home for me was playing JazzFest 2014. JazzFest was always part of my life growing up in New Orleans. It's one of those rare things, a local/tourist hybrid. Everybody goes. We all know the tourists are coming, but we can't wait for JazzFest either, because you can't get that kind of food and music in one place anywhere else. The crawfish bread is worth the trip all by itself; to this day, I don't know where to get crawfish bread outside of JazzFest.

It's always been held in the same place, the fairgrounds. When I went as a kid, and we pulled up to the parking lot, people were everywhere. I could see multiple stages, including the main stage.

There's Congo Square (which always brings me back to Africa), the jazz tent, and the gospel tent, where I grew up playing with my dad. There are the smells of fifty different kinds of food: Creole, Cajun, African, gumbo, jambalaya, you name it. There's a sea of people eating, drinking, singing, dancing, and having a great time. JazzFest is a part of me.

I played there for the first time as part of the St. Aug jazz band. Much later, Freestyle Nation played in Congo Square. But when I was invited to play in 2014, I wanted to do something new, because I've never been a traditional New Orleans musician. I wanted to write a song for my mom, with her name in it, and I wanted a New Orleans vibe. That became "New Orleans Girl." The lyrics came easy:

> *Let's start from the beginning, her name was Debra Brown*
> *She caught my daddy's eye and he's still around*
> *Which helps me prove my point, it must be something in the*
>   *water*
> *'Cause forty years later, and he's still glad he caught her*
> *Ooh, I been all over, all over the world*
> *It still ain't nothing like a New Orleans girl*

The second verse was about Kortni, and I kept going with the same idea. I knew it would work because JazzFest is all about keeping people dancing and moving, and me celebrating the city and its women would do that. I brought Ed, Brian, and the whole band to the stage on Congo Square in front of five to ten thousand people. When we were set up and ready to play, I stepped to the mic and said, "I'm a New Orleans boy, and I wrote this for you!" Everybody cheered. Then we started playing, and the crowd went wild.

I had never written a song specifically for an event before. But it worked, and now I play "New Orleans Girl" every time I appear at JazzFest. It's become a classic New Orleans song and a staple in the city. If you come for Mardi Gras, you'll probably hear it. It's funny, because New Orleans was always one of my toughest markets. But on that day, the people were with me, and they've been with me ever since.

~

As being back in New Orleans became normal again, I started to notice something going on in the music community. A new, younger generation of musicians was on its way up, they knew I was home, and they were looking to me for answers.

The same factors that made me want to leave the city were still there. As long as I could remember, the scene had been all about live performance and jazz. But now there was a younger generation of musicians who wanted to record and innovate, and who didn't grow up on jazz. They grew up on Frank Ocean, the rapper and R&B singer from New Orleans. I met with some of them and we talked, and it was obvious they didn't have an outlet for their music. The scene was still very small, and the message was, "If you have big dreams, get out." My being back seemed to confirm that it was okay for them to be there.

Suddenly, I realized that all these kids were looking at me as a leader. They saw me as someone who was in one of the biggest bands in the world, who had signed with Young Money, toured the globe, and been nominated for Grammys. They looked up to me. It dawned on me that they were a bunch of little PJs, and they wanted me to teach them. I thought, *Why aren't you doing anything about this?*

Thinking back to the Apache Café, I started an open mic with my friend Gio called Sound Bytes to give players a platform. I also started Morton Records, but I realized that building a label and signing people wasn't necessarily the best way to help. I wanted these young players to be independent and make their own way, like I did. So what I mostly did was give advice. They came to me and asked about their ideas, and I made suggestions—where to find musicians or singers, places to record, how to build out songs, stuff like that.

But I'm not for everybody. I usually take the road less traveled, and I knew some young musicians wouldn't want to follow me. That's cool. I want to be a leader for the ones who will. I'm drawn to artists who are incomplete. I'm drawn to artists whose ideas need to be developed, because that's when everybody passes them over. That's when I can help. I liked being a leader for those people. But I wanted to be more than a mentor, because too many mentors just sit and watch from afar. I wanted to lead by example. If my experience has taught me anything, it's that you learn things by doing them, and when you do, a lot of times you realize you already have the answers.

There was only one way I knew how to lead by example. I had to make another record.

~

I decided to do a mixtape of a New Orleans form of hip-hop called *bounce*. Bounce was born in New Orleans dance clubs and features a lot of call-and-response (common in preaching) and up-tempo beats. It reminds me of what go-go is to Washington DC, a regional beat with the same drums and kind of the same rhythm, but with different melodies on top.

I still meant to quit music and open my sneaker store, but first I wanted to do this little side project. I'd been planning to give "New Orleans Girl" to someone else, but instead I started playing around with it using bounce beats. It was like I was making party music.

Then a friend of mine heard the music and said, "You should put that out," and I got excited. Next thing you know, I'm releasing a mixtape called *Bounce & Soul, Volume 1*. It had six of my older tunes on it, remixed as bounce tunes, along with a funny intro from producer and DJ Mannie Fresh, a rambling, entertaining interlude from radio host Wild Wayne, and two interludes from Mack Maine. I employed some of the best sounds from my previous records, like Lil Wayne's vocal on "Lover" and Stevie Wonder's harmonica on "Only One." I also featured some New Orleans legends: Trombone Shorty on "New Orleans Girl," Juvenile on "Work It Out," 5th Ward Weebie on "I Need Your Love," and Dee-1 on "Don't Ever Leave."

Suddenly, music was fun again. There was no pressure, expectations, or worrying about sales or hits. I was just making great beats with friends. The songs weren't new; they were just fun collaborations that I didn't overthink. That project was like my homecoming. I had wanted to make something that would tell everybody that I was home. *Bounce & Soul* was it.

Even the marketing was fun. I launched Morton Records, envisioning it as New Orleans's Motown, and partnered with the PJ's Coffee chain (which some people think I own; I don't) to distribute copies of the CD. You couldn't download the tracks, but if you wanted to hear *Bounce & Soul*, you could come to a PJ's location and get a CD for free. I did some meet and greets and signings at PJ's, and I even enjoyed those. *Bounce & Soul* pulled me out of the funk I had been in since after *New Orleans* came out.

Now I couldn't wait to get back into the studio, but I decided I was done playing the part of the tortured independent artist. If I was gonna make one more record, I wouldn't care about trends or sales or hits. I didn't have to answer to industry people or promoters. I was gonna make the coolest thing I could make just for myself. I was the only audience that mattered. I would do what made me happy and answer to nobody. I would get everything I wanted, no compromises, and if the record flopped, it flopped.

That project was *Gumbo*.

~

One of my favorite books is Malcolm Gladwell's *The Tipping Point*, and I love the subtitle: *How Little Things Can Make a Big Difference*. I didn't change much in making *Gumbo*, or so I thought at the time. I just made the record I wanted to make.

I had already written the song "First Began," but now I needed to focus on writing new material. Other than "Claustrophobic," I hadn't written anything new in three years. But the songs started to flow, and most were songs about life, not the love songs I usually wrote. I had been studying Marvin Gaye's catalog, and I realized that early in his career he had produced almost all love songs. Then he made his *What's Going On* album and got real about issues like racism and violence. I wanted this record to be my *What's Going On*. I wanted to write about real things and not shy away from controversy.

"Sticking to My Guns" is about me staying true to myself in the face of pressure to conform. "They Gon' Wanna Come" is about people coming around with their hand out only after you're successful. I wrote "Everything's Gonna Be Alright" to inspire people who are facing tough times. "Go Thru Your Phone" is about conflict in a relationship. "Religion" was me calling out religious folks for hypocrisy. I also wanted to remake the Bee Gees' "How Deep Is Your Love," which I had always loved.

Because I was mixing together songs about different subjects, I decided to call the record *Gumbo*. Gumbo is a mixture of all this different stuff that makes one beautiful dish, and I wanted this album to be one beautiful dish. I made *Gumbo* on pure instinct, and I had more fun in the studio than I'd had in a long time. *Gumbo* was the first album I ever worked on in New Orleans, and it was very different from working in Atlanta or Los Angeles. Nobody cared that I was working on something new, because New Orleans isn't an industry town. I wasn't worried about paying for a tour or a band, meeting a deadline or producing a song that would chart. Recording time became play time. If a musical idea brought me joy, it went on the record.

Right away, I decided *Gumbo* would have only nine songs, because some of the greatest albums in pop music history, like *Purple Rain* and *Thriller*, have only had nine cuts. I made the demos at home so I could get the feeling and texture right before I brought anyone else in. When I was ready, I realized that I had never recorded in New Orleans, and I ended up at The Parlor Recording Studio, which I liked so much that I eventually tried to buy it. It's a warehouse that was converted into a beautiful state-of-the-art studio. The inside was a mixture of red cloth walls and wood floors, with a gorgeous vintage Neve mixing console that the owner clearly spent a lot of money on. I loved that console. Playing instruments through it gives the sound a warm, old-school feel, like the kind you get with old tube amplifiers.

The live room at The Parlor was huge; you could get a full band in there all at once. Ben Kane was there as the engineer, and I brought back the usual suspects, Brian and Ed, along with DJ Raymond on bass, Alvin Ford Jr. on drums, and Chris Payton on guitar. I brought in rapper Pell, BJ the Chicago Kid, and The Hamiltones—R&B singer Anthony Hamilton's backup group—to help out. But I kept the sound simple. Most of the tracks had keyboard, guitar, bass, and drums, and that was it. I included sax or trumpet on a few tunes, and I brought in Matt Jones to take the strings up a notch. I had been listening to a lot of Frank Sinatra and I wanted that big, lush sound.

There wasn't anything at stake, so the recording had a feeling of looseness. I had my three core songs—"Claustrophobic," "First Began," and "Sticking to My Guns"—so I just had to fill in the blanks. That's how I make records. I ask, "What's missing?" One day, I had this idea in my head, and I asked Alvin and the other guys in the studio about the concept of "Go Thru Your Phone" before I wrote it. I wasn't sure about it. Who writes a song about scrolling through a phone? I asked them, "Would you go through your girl's phone if you could, or would you rather not know?" They all said the same thing: "Nah, man, I wouldn't even want to see it." Once I heard that, I knew I had a hit, because most men agree that anything they found going through their girl's phone wouldn't be worth the trouble they got.

Gumbo came out on April 14, 2017, to some of the best reviews I've ever gotten. Warryn Campbell posted on Instagram that *Gumbo* was "the album of the decade." The record didn't crack the *Billboard 200* or have a charting single, but that didn't matter as much as it had in the past. One reason was that I had signed with Empire Distribution, Records and Publishing, Inc., a fairly new company out of San Francisco, to handle distribution, and *Gumbo* was doing very well in streams.

The other reason not having a hit didn't bother me was that I'd made the record I wanted. My songs reflected the conversations people were having. I took more artistic risks and captured my entire vision. I hadn't worried about commercial prospects at all. With *Gumbo*, making music was fun again, and I'm sure people felt that.

(By the way, my favorite place in New Orleans for actual gumbo is always home. There was a restaurant in New Orleans East called Sassafras that made great gumbo, but it's not there anymore. I grew up on thin, almost soupy, broth and most restaurants make it too thick.)

~

Once *Gumbo* dropped, the obvious move was to tour. So, on June 23, 2017, I announced that the *Gumbo World Tour* would start June 30 in New Orleans, then move to Australia, and then travel all over the United States. We'd play thirty dates in all. If this was going to be my last tour, I was gonna make it one for the books!

From the first show, the tour was fire. I connected with this top executive named John Dee Hammond, the longtime manager and best friend of the singer, songwriter, and record producer Maxwell. God bless him, John told me he had a smaller sub-agency within his bigger company, and that small agency had a junior agent named Garrett. John promised me that Garrett was really hungry and suggested I try him out as a booking agent for the tour. I loved the idea of working with a guy who was hungry and motivated. Garrett joined the team.

Dude was amazing. He had connections with all the venues I wanted to play. Suddenly, we were getting booked at terrific venues I'd never played before, and we went to work. We played five dates in Melbourne, Australia, and then crisscrossed the United States—San Diego, LA, Seattle, Detroit, Chicago, Philadelphia, Nashville, Memphis, New York—and wrapped by playing Stockholm, London, and Paris. It was incredible.

This tour *felt* different, too. The energy was spiritual and intense. People were singing along with "Claustrophobic" and cheering so loudly that we could barely hear ourselves. Ed, Brian, and I would look at one another onstage and I could tell we were all thinking the same thing: *What did we do differently?* This was just us putting on our usual great live show. But something had changed.

For one thing, audiences were getting bigger. The industry was changing. Streaming had become a force and it leveled the playing field. But there was more. On past tours, we would take a few singles off the latest record, mix in some of my older songs, throw in a few covers, and build a set list. On the *Gumbo* tour, people were requesting every song from the album. That had never happened. If we didn't play one of the songs, like "Go Thru Your Phone," they would shout their disappointment.

I think the real reason people reacted to *Gumbo* with so much passion was that I hadn't played it safe. In writing and recording, I only made creative choices that challenged me, excited me, or spoke to my soul. I wasn't worried about what anybody else thought, so I made a work of art that was just for me. Why not? I had nothing to lose. Whatever happened, happened. Ironically, that was what put my career back on track.

~

The 2017 Grammy nominations came out in November, and to my surprise, I had been nominated for two awards: Best R&B Album for *Gumbo*, and Best R&B Song for "First Began." I could hardly believe it. I didn't have a label like Young Money flexing on my behalf; I was an independent, and back then, independent artists didn't get Grammy nominations. This was proof—proof that the music industry was evolving, but also proof that forgetting about commercial considerations and listening to the authentic voice in my head and heart might just be my ticket to real success.

Suddenly, artists reached out to me about *Gumbo* to support me and tell me how much they loved the music. I got interview requests from the music press and the mainstream press. *Gumbo* still hadn't gotten any radio airplay, but the Grammy nominations changed that. Ghazi Shami, the founder of Empire, my distributor, called me. He apologized for not taking notice of me sooner, which made me laugh because I was used to not being noticed. But Ghazi said, "You know, you're Empire's first Grammy nominee," and he told me what a big deal that was.

I replied, "Well, now that 'First Began' is nominated for Best R&B Song, maybe we should go to radio." I was half joking, but Ghazi took me seriously. He decided to get more involved and we strengthened our relationship. Empire put money behind radio airplay, and just like that, "First Began" was on the radio.

A Grammy nomination creates heat like nothing else. When you're nominated, everybody wants to talk to you. All of a sudden, you can book venues you were never able to book before. It's like being engaged, and like being engaged, it's temporary. Once the Grammys broadcast, unless you win, you turn back into a pumpkin. The Grammys would be awarded on January 28, 2018, so I had maybe two months as "Grammy-nominated PJ Morton," and I wanted to take advantage of the spotlight while it was on me. I didn't like my chances because I was up against Bruno Mars in both of my categories, but since I had nothing to lose, why not do something special to keep the attention on *Gumbo*?

The answer was in the incredible live response to the *Gumbo* tour. There wasn't time to tour, but I could make a live version of the *Gumbo* record and capture that same energy. My past live records, like *Live in LA*, had included songs from multiple albums. I had never recorded every song from one album live in concert before. This time, that's what I would do. We would just play the songs from *Gumbo*.

That was good, but it wasn't enough. Then I had it. We would record *Gumbo* live in New York (where the Grammys would broadcast from Madison Square Garden) on Grammy weekend! The entire industry would be in town for the sixtieth anniversary of the Grammys, and we had this hot record, so why not? I even told my manager, Wade, to underplay the recording session. "Let's not hype it," I said. I wanted to create a special event and have people wondering what was going on behind closed doors. That was the start of *Gumbo Unplugged*.

I booked the acclaimed studio Power Station at BerkleeNYC, previously known as Avatar Studios, where superstars like Madonna, Lady Gaga, Bruce Springsteen, Herbie Hancock, Bobby McFerrin, and Paul McCartney had recorded. I brought in my longtime band and recruited some other world-class talent: the Matt Jones Orchestra directed by Matt Jones, Keyon Harrold, BJ the Chicago Kid, Lecrae, The Hamiltones, and singer-songwriter Yebba (who did the duet with me on "How Deep Is Your Love").

This was a live album, so I invited fans, brought in a camera crew to shoot a "making of" video, and packed the room. I was a little disappointed because I wanted the room to look like the Beatles' famous taping of "All You Need Is Love," with the Rolling Stones wandering in the background and fans sitting all over the room and floor, but the New York fire marshal wouldn't allow that. In the end, we were allowed to have only thirty people in the studio, because I already had a sixteen-person orchestra.

Finally we started playing, and the result exceeded my wildest expectations. Not only did we blow the doors off the studio, but the entire record was one long take. We didn't do any overdubs. It was magical. It's the human in it. You let go of any need to produce or be perfect and you can capture an in-the-moment passion and spirit that can't be re-created.

I also wanted to extend the conversations on some of the songs, so we had fun and let the songs breathe. "Religion" ran more than five minutes. "Everything's Gonna Be Alright" turned into a seven-minute call-and-response gospel jam session. *Gumbo Unplugged* was everything I wanted it to be and more.

~

I lost both Grammys. No big deal. In March 2018, I released *Gumbo Unplugged*, and in April the band hit the road. Before long, it was obvious that people were even more fired up for *Gumbo Unplugged* than they had been for the original record. The songs were all the same, but fans cheered and screamed everywhere we went, and sang along with *everything*. At one show, a man proposed to his girlfriend (she said yes). The vibe was pure love and appreciation.

Meanwhile, the video of me and Yebba duetting on "How Deep Is Your Love" went viral and turned the song into a single without us ever releasing an actual single. We had a great thing going, so we just kept touring until we were all *Gumbo*-ed out.

In the end, we toured with just those nine songs for nearly *three years*. *Gumbo Unplugged* felt like a new record because the energy was dialed up so high, but ultimately it was still those same nine songs I wrote for *Gumbo*. Somehow, audiences never got tired of hearing them, and we never got tired of playing them. To my surprise, I also had a wealth of new musical ideas that I hadn't used yet. It was the first time I had felt so creative.

I also loved the community I was building with my fans. When I spoke to them about what they cared about, they responded. I had become a tastemaker. I wasn't the biggest, but the biggest were paying attention to what I was doing. I wasn't sure what to do after *Gumbo Unplugged*, but that was okay. I was enjoying songwriting and producing again, and I was doing what I wanted to do. I was back.

Kortni always tells me that no matter what the disappointment is, I find a way to reset and try one more time. I might say, "I can't do this anymore," but I find a way back. I think that's the key to happiness. Do what you believe in and don't quit. Things can change, even when you're not paying attention.

Chapter Fourteen

Be Like Water

The success of *Gumbo Unplugged* opened a lot of doors in 2018, one of which was an invitation to play a Tiny Desk concert on National Public Radio. The Tiny Desk series got its start back in 2008 when *All Songs Considered* host Bob Boilen and NPR Music editor Stephen Thompson went to the South by Southwest Music Festival but got sick of not being able to hear the music. They made the semi-joke that a folk singer named Laura Gibson should just perform at Boilen's desk—which, one month later, she did. Just like that, a tradition was created.

Since then, nearly one thousand Tiny Desk concerts have happened, featuring lots of obscure artists looking for their big break, but also some big names like Post Malone, Usher, and Ed Sheeran. On July 2, 2018, it was my turn, and I did a very PJ-like thing: I managed to squeeze the entire Matt Jones Orchestra, backup singers The Amours, Ed, Brian, and my Fender Rhodes keyboard behind Bob's desk and turn the suddenly crowded space into a mini–*Gumbo Unplugged*. We performed "Claustrophobic," "Go

Thru Your Phone," and "First Began," for an enormous radio audience, another example of the surprising impact my live record was having.

Another door opened when I got a call from Tyler Perry about appearing in a movie he was directing called *Nobody's Fool*. As I've said, I've known Tyler since I was a kid, back when he was acting in plays, long before he became a movie mogul and a billionaire. He used to carry me through our church on his shoulders when I was little, and because he's such a tall man, I would feel twenty feet high. I didn't recognize the number when he called, but when I answered, the first thing he said was, "Sorry, I think I bumped your head when you were seven years old."

His new studio wasn't fully open yet, but they were filming *Nobody's Fool* there. He told me the movie had a scene in a jazz club, and he wanted me to bring my band and play "How Deep Is Your Love" during the scene. Sure, why not? I took Big Ed, Brian, and my band and went to the studio, where they had built an entire jazz club set. Tyler came into the room, wrapped me in a big hug, and brought big energy with him. I hadn't talked to him in years, and he had become larger than life, but he made me feel super comfortable.

We got in place, waited for the crew to set the lights and position the cameras, and then when Tyler said, "Action," we played. I think we played the song three times, and that was it. Now I'm immortalized in *Nobody's Fool*. I think I watched my scene on a plane once.

It's been great to know Tyler. Having a front-row seat to watch someone build what he's built from scratch had an effect on me. He's truly a self-made man. Tyler Perry Studios in Atlanta is one of the most successful entertainment companies in the country. He's produced major movies, *The Walking Dead*, and so much more on his lot. I was there at the very beginning when he was just figuring it out. To watch him go from rags to riches made me believe I could succeed independently. I followed a lot of the blueprint that he set down.

The year kept getting better when Maroon was invited to headline the halftime show for Super Bowl LIII the following February. That was a rough year in the NFL, because that's the year lots of artists boycotted the halftime show to protest the league's treatment of Colin Kaepernick. In case you don't remember, Kaepernick was the Black San Francisco 49ers quarterback who took a knee at a game in 2016 to protest police brutality against people of color, kicking off a huge controversy.

Major artists like Jay-Z, Cardi B, and Rihanna refused to participate in the show. When Maroon accepted, a petition was organized calling for us to drop out of the show, and we were accused of siding with the league over the players. As the only Black person in the band, I caught a lot of the attention, which I didn't want.

It was bittersweet, because I'd waited my whole life to play the Super Bowl, and the year we got offered the Super Bowl was the most controversial. I hadn't watched football for the whole year—and I'm a big NFL fan—out of solidarity with the players. I remember Adam calling when I was at the Parlor working on music, and he said, "Bro, we got the Super Bowl!" My first reaction was excitement, followed by *Oh my God, of all years, this year*. But I was going to roll with my band.

Ultimately, I was happy. This was my dream come true. It's a short list of people who have headlined the halftime show. But a strange thing happened. Because the show was so controversial, Maroon didn't do much press leading up to the performance.

We just were kind of chilling. But *Gumbo Unplugged* had been nominated for several Grammys, so I had to do press for that, and because these outlets couldn't get Maroon, I got nothing from the press but questions about the Super Bowl. "What do you think about Kaepernick?" "Do you disagree with his stance, or are you boycotting?" That kind of stuff.

I couldn't get away from it. The guys in the band were grateful, because I was taking some bullets, and I could speak to the situation in a different way as the only Black person in the band. At one point I said something like, "If the players boycotted, the whole thing would be over right now. It's unfair that Kap is boycotting to get his job back but people are asking me to boycott because the NFL wants me to do a job for one game."

Bittersweet is the right word.

~

Preparing to play at the Super Bowl is a massive thing. We rehearsed for weeks in California. We did a sound check and ran through the show multiple times so the techs could get their camera angles the night before. We had a huge stage built. We had to re-create all our pyrotechnics and other effects from our live show. I've never gone through more security clearances—more than going to the White House. The producers wanted approval of everything. We sent them pictures of what we'd be wearing. We were prepared.

The game was played at Mercedes-Benz Stadium in Atlanta, which holds about seventy thousand people. I love football, but you cannot focus on the first half of the game when you're doing the halftime show. The moment and the setting are overwhelming.

We were in the back where the locker rooms are, waiting, and the game was going so fast. Then it was time.

Walking out from the dark tunnel into the light...what can I say? It was nerve-racking and super exciting, because about eighty million people would be watching us. Trust me, you feel the weight of that, because the Super Bowl is the one program that people around the world always watch live. I could feel the attention not just of the seventy thousand screaming fans in the stadium but of all those other millions who would be watching to see if we got the show wrong or right.

The people were hyped and the cheers were deafening as we came on. Thousands of flashes hit me as people took photos with their phones, taking me back for a second to those Full Gospel events at the Superdome when I was a kid. We took our places, and we started playing. We had been rehearsing this show for months, so we knew every part like clockwork, and it went off without a hitch. But even though we played for thirteen minutes, adrenaline made it feel like two minutes. My kids and Kortni were there, and after we'd finished, I got to go to the box with them, relax, and finally watch the rest of the halftime show.

It was spectacular. Travis Scott was a part of it, Big Boi from OutKast, Sleepy Brown...it was like a celebration. We were happy with it. The bittersweet part was that no matter what we did, we were going to take some flack because of the boycott. Actually, the press mostly talked about Adam taking his shirt off, which he does half the time anyway.

I've played TV shows. I played Rock in Rio, in front of one hundred thousand people. The Super Bowl was the biggest thing I've ever done, no question. The impact of those millions of viewers is incredible. One of my friends, who's written a bunch of songs for Usher, told me that one of his albums that had been considered a flop went double platinum after the Super Bowl because Usher sang one of his songs at the halftime show in 2024. That's power and impact, and you feel that when you're on that stage.

I don't regret that we did it. I'm happy. It's a short list of people who've ever played that show, and I'm honored to be one of them.

~

As great as the Super Bowl was, it takes a back seat to what happened on February 10, 2019. A couple of months earlier, the nominations for the sixty-first Grammy Awards had been announced, and to my shock, *Gumbo Unplugged* was nominated for three awards: Best R&B Album, Best R&B Performance for "First Began," and Best Traditional R&B Performance for "How Deep Is Your Love."

For a second, I thought somebody was punking me! Live performances rarely get Grammy nods, and "First Began" was a repeat nomination, since the same song had been nominated in 2017 (albeit in a different category) after it appeared on *Gumbo*. What?

This was yet another clue that I had hit on something profound with *Gumbo Unplugged*. Something—the love, the freedom, the passion, the joy—was hitting people hard and making them look at my music in a new way. But while I enjoyed being nominated, I didn't expect to win. I had been nominated three times before as a solo artist and three times with Maroon (we picked up a fourth in 2018, Best Pop Duo/Group Performance for "Girls Like You"), but left empty-handed, so I was used to it.

I have never chased Grammys, and I wasn't about to start. Winning a Grammy would have been a by-product of doing work that I loved. And anyway, it really was an honor just to be nominated. I know that's a cliché, but it's legit. So much new music comes out every single day that just to be noticed and respected is an accomplishment. Plus, everything about *Gumbo* and *Gumbo Unplugged* had left me feeling great; I couldn't imagine that winning a Grammy would feel better. I went to the ceremony in February trying not to get my hopes up.

Kortni didn't want to go at all. When something hurts me, she gets mad on my behalf, and she'd watched me get crushed every other time I lost. She didn't want us to travel to Los Angeles and get all dressed up, only to sit through another night of disappointment. Of course, we ended up going. It was me, Kortni, Brian Cockerham, and Wade Jordan, my manager, sitting together at the Staples Center, waiting.

We were at the pre-show, where most of the awards are handed out. The evening show, the one that's on TV, is where they announce the handful of major awards, like Record of the Year and Album of the Year. But in categories like classical, jazz, and R&B, you have to get up at ten in the morning and get ready.

The R&B categories usually come late in the game. Category after category came up, winners were announced, and artists gave their speeches. Finally, Best R&B Performance was up, and "First Began" lost to "Best Part" by H.E.R. featuring Daniel Caesar. Immediately, I thought, *Here we go again.*

A bunch of other awards were given out, and I thought, *Now you're just dragging it out.* Finally, we got to Best Traditional R&B Performance, and they ran through the nominees: "How Deep Is Your Love" by me and Yebba; "Bet Ain't Worth the Hand" by Leon Bridges; "Don't Fall Apart on Me Tonight" by Bettye LaVette; "Honest" by MAJOR; and "Made for Love" by Charlie Wilson featuring Lalah Hathaway.

Then the presenter said, "And the Grammy goes to . . . we have a tie." Then a long pause. Meanwhile, I was dying.

"Leon Bridges . . ."

Okay . . . and?

" . . . and PJ Morton!"

When they said my name, it was surreal. It didn't feel real. It felt like I was in a dream. Everything went silent for a second. *Did they just say my name? Did I just win a Grammy after all this time?*

Kortni let out the loudest scream I've ever heard her make. She never screams. She'll tell you. It was like the pain and years of hard work and broken promises all came out of her. But I didn't hear her scream until I watched the video. Meanwhile, Brian, who's been with me forever, went crazy. Then I figured I'd better walk up to the microphone and accept my Grammy. I saw Yebba come up to the microphone beside me. I looked out into that brightly lit theater and I could see Kortni and Brian. But it wasn't just them; everybody was cheering for us. These were my peers. They know the people they vote for, and there was nothing but love in that room.

I don't think Leon Bridges was there, because he didn't come up to accept. They went straight to me, and I didn't have any notes. I should have prepared something, but every time I did, I lost. Now I was trying to figure out what to say. *Make sure you thank Kortni. Make sure you thank God.* In the end I thanked God, Kortni, Wade, and Tanya. I think I thanked my band, Ed, and Brian. Then they went right on to the next category.

Somebody whisked us backstage so the official photographer could take pictures of me with the Grammy. My Grammy hadn't been engraved yet, obviously, so they gave me a fake one that was surprisingly heavy. Everyone was congratulating me every step of the way, but I barely noticed; I was still in shock. *Wow, that really just happened.* Then I started seeing other artists back there who had just won and I started telling them, "Congratulations." It felt so good to be part of the winners' club! Then they took me down the hall to talk to the press.

The questions were stuff like, "This is your first time winning. What was it like?" Most of the press didn't know who I was; they were asking as a courtesy. But there was one guy from an R&B magazine who knew me, so when the PR rep asked, "Does anybody have any more questions?" he raised his hand and said, "PJ, how do you feel?" I don't remember what I said, but it was comforting.

Eventually, I met Kortni, Brian, and everybody outside of the theater and we just started screaming and cheering and hugging each other. Ironically, in previous years I had planned a little dinner or something for after the ceremony, but this year, after all those losses, I decided not to plan anything. Now I had won, and I had no way to celebrate! Fortunately, my band was in LA for a gig, so we all had drinks together upstairs at our hotel. I still couldn't believe it. *Surreal* really is the only word that works. In a second, my life had changed. I felt really good. I felt like I had stuck to who I was and had finally been rewarded for it.

All my Grammys felt great, but not many things in music can compare to that first one. It was more than the award. I had told myself the award didn't matter but I was wrong. It was validation. It was belonging. It was acceptance. I belonged to the fraternity now. *You recognized me.* That mattered to me. There's a reason artists get up there and cry when they win. You can't remember what to say because it matters. Respect from your peers means more than anything.

In that moment, *everything* became worth it.

~

Somehow, February 2019 just kept getting better. Right after the Grammys, I played at the Kennedy Center for the first time as part of a celebration of Valentine's Day. Talk about an honor! I brought my own orchestra and played a set of mostly love songs, including songs from *Gumbo* and one of my staples, "Where Everybody Knows Your Name," from *Cheers*. But that wasn't the highlight of the night.

The highlight came when I saw my mom and dad in the audience. I hadn't known if they were going to be in DC or not, so when I saw them, I got up from the grand piano I'd been playing, walked to the edge of the stage in my tux, pointed at my dad, and said, "My dad is here. I want my dad." This was more role reversal, as well as a little good-natured revenge. He'd been doing the same to me my whole life! So often, during Sunday services, he had said, "Come on PJ, come up here and play," or "Come up here and sing for us, PJ." This was my chance to turn the tables on him.

I didn't want to embarrass him, but I also knew without a doubt that he would be ready. He's spent his life in church, and church is not about preparation. Church is about being in the moment. I knew he probably wanted to sing, and I was positive he had been singing the whole show under his breath anyway. So when I pointed at him, he came up and took the mic, just like that.

Everybody went crazy—until that moment, they hadn't known he was there.

Inside and outside the gospel community, my dad is beloved. Fans who knew me from my solo work or from Maroon saw him and suddenly it was like, "Bishop Morton is the man!" I went back to the piano, the house started cheering and clapping, my band started playing "Everything's Gonna Be Alright," and my dad, standing in front of the orchestra pit in his tuxedo, started singing.

The man could still bring it! "Everything's Gonna Be Alright" was perfect because it's a call-and-response song, and call-and-response is what preaching is all about. My dad was taking the whole Kennedy Center to church, and the place was on fire! They don't really get stuff like that there; that's not the vibe. But my invitation had been part of an effort to bring different musical influences to the Kennedy Center, and that's exactly what we did.

Dad absolutely killed it. We'd been planning to end with "How Deep Is Your Love," but this was the end of the show. Everybody was on their feet. It was crazy. After we'd finished, people were buzzing: *Oh my God, your dad. Who knew he was going to be here?* Even the people who didn't know him were blown away. It was a special moment.

After that, I've never passed up an opportunity to hand my dad the mic. I sold out the Orpheum in New Orleans on Black Friday of 2023, something that's very rare because New Orleans is a "walk-up city." No matter who you are, your shows won't sell out early, but if you have fans who love you, they will walk up thirty minutes before showtime and you'll sell out. I had a full house that night, and once again I handed my dad the mic that night to sing "Everything's Gonna Be Alright." He killed again, like he always does. People love those moments, but he still seems shocked by the response. It warms my heart. He still comes up to me after New Orleans shows and says things like, "Man, they really love you. This is crazy."

~

Winning the Grammy changed everything about my career and my life. My friends celebrated by having a second line band meet me when I arrived back in New Orleans. It was the best homecoming I'd ever gotten. I did *The Daily Show with Trevor Noah* and played at The Shed, a new cultural center, on opening night for "Soundtrack of America," a Black music festival put together by heavyweights like Quincy Jones.

I also got to work on a new album. Basically, I had written and performed the same nine songs for the previous three years, so I had plenty of material in my head. I was ready to write and record, so I said, "Let's go again." Out of that came the album *Paul*. I go by PJ, but Paul is the name I was born with, and it's who I'll always be.

I brought in more first-class talent—Tobe Nwigwe, Jazmine Sullivan, Rapsody, JoJo, and Angela Rye—and recorded at The Parlor. *Paul* was a mix of R&B and soul, it came out on August 9, 2019, and it gave me my first top ten single on the *Billboard* Adult R&B Songs chart, "Say So." I had written the song already, but it didn't feel like a good fit for *Gumbo*. After the Grammy, I reworked it and got JoJo, who's a fantastic R&B singer, to join me on vocals. The result was my biggest song to date. I finally had a radio hit only fourteen years after I started!

Making *Paul* was fun. I was finally where I wanted to be in my career. I had received the recognition I craved, and good things were happening everywhere I looked. I made that record from a place of comfort and joy. I think *Paul* is still the only album that I made feeling that way, and it shows in the music.

When the 2020 Grammys came around, I was nominated in three categories: Best R&B Album for *Paul*, Best Traditional R&B Performance for "Built for Love," and Best R&B Song for "Say So." But that day was bittersweet, because it was the day Kobe Bryant, his daughter, Gianna, and seven other people died in a helicopter crash. I found out right before I went to the ceremony, which was in the Staples Center—Kobe's house when he played for the LA Lakers. So that was weighing heavily on everybody.

I got the news that morning when I was getting dressed at my hotel. Peyton, just eight years old, was my guest that year, because Kortni didn't come. The shadow of what had happened to Kobe was deep. I was with my own daughter. It was a lot. But we went to the ceremony and did our best to enjoy it. I was up against Chris Brown and H.E.R. for Best R&B Album, so I figured I couldn't win and I was right. Best Traditional R&B Performance, which I thought was my best chance to win, went to Lizzo. Two of the three, back to back.

I was fine, but I could see that Peyton was taking it a little hard. I leaned over to her in her fancy dress and explained. I said, "Now, Pey Pey, somebody has to lose. Everybody's good at music at this point—" I was sitting there explaining it to her, telling her why it was important to be a good loser, and I heard the presenter read the winner for Best R&B Song:

"PJ Morton for 'Say So'!"

The next lesson is canceled. Just forget what I said. We'll come back to it. I grabbed Peyton by the hand and led her up to the mic. When I got there, I made the whole audience say, "Hey, Pey Pey!" They shouted back, "Hey, Pey Pey!" and even though she was embarrassed, she waved. It was the cutest thing. That was special, being with Peyton up there. She did a little dance with me backstage, and we took pictures together on the red carpet. That'll be with her forever. It'll be with me forever, too.

As I look back at that year, I can't help but be humbled by everything that took place. It was hard to believe how fast my fortunes had changed. Within twelve months, I went from being a three-time Grammy runner-up to a two-time winner. Those wins changed my professional life. I was still the same artist and songwriter, but now I had the Grammy seal of approval. People who might not have paid attention to me before took my calls now. I was able to enjoy opportunities and exposure I'd never had before. But I didn't let the success change who I was or how I took care of business. That was one of the things that helped me make the most of what came next.

Part Three

Encore

Chapter Fifteen

Everything's Gonna Be All Right

What came next was COVID-19. How did I "make the most" of that? COVID let me know what a crazy pace I'd been maintaining. By the start of 2020, I hadn't stopped working since recording *Gumbo* in 2016. I was going so hard because once I saw the reaction to *Gumbo*, it became an experiment. What would happen to my career if I literally gave everything—if I just put my head down and went for it? I decided to try it, and I saw the results with *Gumbo Unplugged*.

After that, I got carried away. If I had one day between a Maroon tour and a PJ Morton tour, I would work. I did a whole US tour with Maroon, took one day home with Kortni and the kids, and then went to Asia to do a solo thing. It became manic. My attitude was *I've got to keep going. I've got to keep going.* I had never had such momentum behind my career. This was what I had wanted my entire life. I was finally getting attention for making the music I loved, and I was afraid the post-Grammy energy would die out. So I kept going. I didn't realize how crazy it was because I didn't take a moment to think about it.

I could have gone on for a while. After *Gumbo* and *Gumbo Unplugged*, I wasn't burned out; I was charged up. I had made *Paul*, and now I was ready to do another live thing. For years, my friends had said to me, "You should just do a piano record," but I didn't want to. I still didn't like being the only one in the spotlight. Then I did this show on YouTube called *The Terrell Show*. I brought my piano, played keys, sang, and played word association games. The episode was very popular, and many of the comments were things like, "I loved just hearing his songs like this, just him on piano."

Right after New Year's 2020, I invited friends to join me in the studio. They didn't know what they were coming for; I just said, "Y'all come to Conway Studios in LA and just react how you react." The only people who got a heads-up were artists I would ask to sing: Alex Isley, who did "How Deep Is Your Love" with me; JoJo, who did "Say So"; and The Walls Group, who sang on "Let Go." I didn't tell them exactly what they were going to be doing, so it was really a great vibe.

We cut the record in one take, straight through. That's become my signature. I don't like doing a lot of takes. If you do that, the sound starts to become contrived. I'm all about spontaneity. Even if it's not as perfect as what you might want, I like the feeling better. I think perfection is imperfect in music. Imperfection is what makes it a vibe, makes it special. I want to be well rehearsed, locked in, and tight, but there's room for humanity. That's the sweet spot.

I released *The Piano Album* on Valentine's Day 2020. We had no idea that, a few months later, the world would shut down, and

The Piano Album would become everybody's soothing, healing pandemic record. But I wasn't done yet.

~

In mid-2019, months before the 2020 Grammys, I decided to give my dad a gift. Through all the years that I had been making secular records, I'd kept my hand in the world of gospel. That summer, I had been writing and producing a record for the great gospel singer Le'Andria Johnson when her team told me they had decided to go in a different direction. No problem; that's the music business. But I loved these songs, and now I had no one to record them.

I started to think about all the gospel tunes I had written and produced for other artists on other labels. If you write a song for someone else and another label releases it, it's never one hundred percent your song, even if you also produce it. Once the recording part is over, the way the label presents and promotes it is out of your hands. Now I had the opportunity to control every part of how those songs went out into the world.

The more I thought about the idea, the more it appealed to me. A gospel record would give me a chance to show people my journey and tell them my larger story while paying tribute to the music I had grown up with. This was also a chance to make my dad, who had never expected me to make a gospel record, very happy. That's how *Gospel According to PJ: From the Songbook of PJ Morton* came to be.

First, I had to choose from the many gospel songs I had written. Once I narrowed the list down to ten songs, I had to find artists who could bring my songs and vision to life. My first try was a shot in the dark. It was July 2019, and the Essence Music Festival, the biggest celebration of Black music and culture in the country, was lighting up the streets of New Orleans like it did every summer. I knew that sisters Erica Atkins-Campbell and Tina Atkins-Campbell—the Grammy-winning, best-selling gospel duo known as Mary Mary—were in town for Essence Fest. They're great friends of mine, so I reached out to them and begged them to come to my studio and record the song I had written for Le'Andria Johnson.

They agreed, even though it was the end of a long day and their voices were tired. They came to my studio, and despite not having recorded in the studio in quite a while, they killed it. The result was "All in His Plan," which would become my first song to reach number one on the *Billboard* Gospel Airplay chart.

With one song down, I reached out to other gospel artists I had worked with. Years earlier, in 2006, I had written a song called "Let Go" for Men of Standard, but they had just put the finishing touches on their new album and didn't have room for another tune. DeWayne Woods recorded the song instead, and it became a massive hit and a Stellar Award winner. Now I ended up bringing in the incredible Smokie Norful to record "Let Go" and mixed it with a recording of another song, "God Can."

With *The Piano Album* out, it started to look like the gospel album was possible—until the world came to a dead stop in March 2020.

~

Maroon was in Colombia in early March and we started hearing about this new virus called COVID-19. A lot of people in Asia were catching it, and a lot of them were dying horribly. Within a few days, our show in Colombia was canceled, and then about thirty minutes later, we got word that the show for the next day in Argentina had also been canceled. International travel was starting to shut down, too, and the tour stopped being as important as getting back to our families.

Kortni and I thought, like so many other people did, that this pandemic—that's what the authorities had started calling it—might last for two weeks. We were so naive. We treated it like a vacation. I said to Reggie, my engineer, "Since we're going to be locked down for two weeks, let's get some of my equipment over to my house and I'll just work from there." I was on a roll; why let a thing like a global plague stop me? I was already doing some early work on what would become my next album, *Watch the Sun*, and I didn't want to slow down.

Then in late March, my laptop crashed. I should have taken it as a sign, but I didn't—not right away. The reality was, I was moving faster than I could think, faster than was good for me. I had been trying to recover a file and I did something I would ordinarily never do: I used a file recovery program. It crashed my system. When I realized what had happened, it was like a heavy weight crashing into my chest. I lost almost everything I had been working on—lyrics, tracks, everything. What I wanted most was all the drum parts that I had built over all those years, but they were gone.

However, my computer crashing actually turned out to be a blessing. I finally had to stop, and I suddenly realized how tired I was. I realized how much of my kids' lives I had missed over the past four years of running from tour to gig to studio. I was a no-joke workaholic. I'm still a workaholic, but now I build in time for other things. It seems strange to say, but the pandemic gave me balance.

One thing I took the time to do was circle back to the gospel album. When I recorded the first few songs, it was still sort of a "maybe" project, a labor of love. But now New Orleans and the entire country were shut down, and bringing artists to my studio was out of the question. Then I thought, *When will I ever have access to all these amazing artists again?* They were all home because of COVID-19, and if they were willing to record in their home studios while I produced remotely, I could actually make the record. I began reaching out to my all-star team of gospel legends.

Kirk Franklin. Commissioned. The Clark Sisters. J. Moss, who produced the first song I ever placed. These and many other top gospel artists had watched me grow up and grow into the musician I had become, and now here I was offering them a chance to create something even though we were all isolated in our homes. Most of them generously said yes. So, over the coming months, working around the distance, technical setbacks, and some people inevitably getting sick, we made the record.

The result was a dream come true, a chronicle of my years in the church and my growth as a songwriter. But it wasn't quite done. Even with all ten tracks recorded, the album needed something else. Then it occurred to me what was missing. It was impossible to talk about my vision of gospel music without talking about my dad.

So I decided to record a conversation with him and cut it into three brief spoken-word interludes: "Dad's Interlude: WEL-COME," "Dad's Interlude: ORIGIN," and "Dad's Interlude: IN CLOSING." They became my favorite parts of the album. Those brief talks tied everything together and brought it all home.

Finally, on August 28, 2020, a year after I'd conceived it, Morton Records and Tyscot Records released *Gospel According to PJ: From the Songbook of PJ Morton* into a frightened world that needed messages of hope and healing…messages that gospel delivers better than just about anything else. At the 63rd Grammys the following winter, it even won the award for Best Gospel Album. I just watched and laughed in amazement. *Three in a row.*

That record represented everything I've become as an artist. I trusted my gut instincts, leaned on people I've come to know and love, and let my authentic voice guide me—all the hallmarks of my music career.

That was the last work I did for months. The pandemic gave me time to take a long look in the mirror at who I was becoming, and I've made some important changes. The way I deal with Kortni is different. The way I deal with the kids is different. Once the gospel record was done, I didn't do anything but dad and home stuff for months. I built shelves and bookcases. I taught Peyton and P3 how to ride bikes. I was fully in dad mode and loving it. I wasn't thinking about music at all. I didn't want to think about it.

~

The next year, 2021, I worked on a song for Jon Batiste called "BOY HOOD," which ended up on his album *We Are.* The song got a Grammy nomination and lost, but the album won Album of the Year at the 2022 ceremony, giving me my fourth Grammy. But more importantly, by the spring of 2021, I was back in the studio working on my next album, *Watch the Sun.*

My computer crash had destroyed the first round of songs that would have been on *Watch the Sun,* but now I was ready to make the record. Everyone—my band, my friends, my colleagues, my longtime musical family—had been cooped up for a year, and we missed each other. We had been playing and touring for so long and were so used to being around each other that I decided I would bring us all together to make my next record.

But this was still the middle of COVID, when not everyone had been vaccinated and people were still dying in overcrowded hospitals by the thousands every day. If we were going to make a record, we had to do it safely. That meant finding a secluded location to record, lodgings close by that were just as isolated, and testing everyone for coronavirus infection not just once but several times. I talked to the players and singers I wanted for *Watch the Sun* and they agreed to what I had in mind. Now I just had to find the right location.

I found and rented Studio in the Country, a famous, secluded recording studio in Bogalusa, Louisiana. This place was legendary. Stevie Wonder had made a record there in the 1970s, *Journey Through the Secret Life of Plants*. Jimmy Buffett, Willie Nelson, and the Neville Brothers all recorded there. It was perfect. I could bring in all my people and we could all live in the area, isolated from the world and the pandemic, and make music. Over the next few weeks, everybody got tested (fortunately, most tested negative), and we all gathered at the house to be together, have fun, and work.

There was as much fun as there was work. It was like being at an adult summer camp. It was the most amazing thing I have ever done. It was just me and my friends with land and a pond and nothing to do but be together and make music. It was heaven. We played spades late into the night, just like when I was at Morehouse. I barbecued. It was beautiful. To make music in that environment was pure freedom. But I also knew I would want to chill after the record was done, because it felt like the end of a chapter for me. So I decided I would pull out all the stops.

I went after and got an incredible list of collaborators: Nas, Stevie Wonder, El DeBarge, JoJo, Wale, Jill Scott, Alex Isley, Mr. TalkBox, Chronixx, Zacardi Cortez, Gene Moore, Samoht, Tim Rogers, and Darrel "MusiqCity" Walls. Most of them recorded their parts remotely and sent them to me for mixing. Like *Gumbo*, the final record was a blend of love songs and life songs. The result was, in my opinion, my masterpiece, at least up to that time.

Watch the Sun was my way of saying, "The sun sets and rises every single day. No matter how dark it gets, at some point the sun's gonna come back." It was a message of hope that was sorely needed as everybody hoped and prayed for the pandemic to end. *Watch the Sun* was released on April 20, 2022, and later that year it would pick up three Grammy nominations: Best R&B Album, Best Gospel Performance/Song for "The Better Benediction," and Best R&B Song for "Please Don't Walk Away." I didn't win any of them, but it was surprising how little the Grammys mattered once I had won one. I'd had the joy of working with my friends again and making music I loved. Winning more Grammys would've just been icing on the cake.

After putting out four records in three years—*Paul, The Piano Album, Gospel According to PJ*, and *Watch the Sun*—I was ready for a long break. I didn't take one. In early 2023, Kortni and I were on vacation in Cabo San Lucas when Lauryn Hill's "The Sweetest Thing" came into my mind out of nowhere. It's a great song with a great vibe, so in the summer I recorded my version of it and released it on YouTube. That's what I love about being independent. I can get inspired, go into the studio, bring that vision to life, and release it to the people in a week. No permission, no schedules, no delays.

Next came *Watch the Sun Live: The Mansion Sessions*. After my experience with *Gumbo Unplugged*, I knew the recipe: bring great people into a studio space to create a warm, infectious vibe, and hit Record. I rented a mansion in LA's San Fernando Valley, brought in an orchestra, a twenty-piece band, and some family members and friends, and we all went to work keeping soul music alive. Fans could hear the record on streaming or watch the session on YouTube. It was one more celebration of family, music, and authenticity.

After *The Mansion Sessions*, I was spent. I thought I might be finished making commercial albums. I'd been looking at the soul group Frankie Beverly & Maze as a blueprint. They haven't put out a new record in thirty years, but they're beloved by the culture, have an amazing live show, tour consistently, and continue to sell out venues. I could see myself doing that. For years, it had been one foot in front of the other, and my feet were sore. I wouldn't quit music, because there was more I wanted to do, and more I wanted to say. I thought I could be very happy performing live and producing.

But as you've probably guessed, things didn't work out that way.

~

In October 2023, my fascination with Africa grew stronger than my desire to take it easy, and I went to Africa. I went to make a new album—to write new songs, meet African musicians and artists—and also to play live and learn about the culture and people. I'd been to Morocco and Egypt with Maroon; we performed at a festival in Morocco and did a show in front of the pyramids in Giza. But that's not Black Africa. I had never been to the place where my ancestors were taken from. I was supposed to go in 2020, but we all know what happened then. This was my chance.

My partner, the Empire label, is very successful in Africa, and they'd been asking me for a while if I wanted to do any collaborations with African artists. Then Wade, my manager, started talking to me about *Graceland*, Paul Simon's album. It was incredible, but Simon also got accused of cultural appropriation. Finally, I said, "If I'm going to do it, I want to spend time there and go to multiple places." In the end, we agreed I would spend thirty days in Africa and see if I could write an entire new record in that time. What could I create in thirty days? I liked the idea of the challenge. We would also bring a cameraman and record a documentary about the experience.

The thing is, Africa is *huge*. A nonstop flight from Johannesburg, South Africa, to Lagos, Nigeria, takes about six and a half hours. This was a major undertaking. Not only did I want to make an album, but I wanted to eat the local food, meet the artists and creatives, do radio, do TV, go to the clubs—I wanted to immerse myself. I would also conduct an experiment: I would not write anything before I went, and I would not write anything after I got back. This album would be fully created in Africa. I had no idea what I was doing, but I trusted my instincts. We booked some shows so we'd have a foundation.

Flying from New Orleans to Cape Town, South Africa, took more than seventeen hours. When we arrived, one of the first things that struck me was that Cape Town was beautiful. It was mountains and green hills and blue ocean, and when I thought of

Africa, that was not what I had imagined. We slept off the jet lag on that first night, and the next day I went to this little studio. I had part of my band with me—Ed, Brian, Reggie (my engineer), and Brent (my tour manager). I didn't know what I needed, so I just took a few people who could help me. I didn't even have any songs. But I could *feel* that I was in Africa. I was seeing my people. It was the first time that everybody looked like me. People were walking up to me and saying, "Welcome home." That hit me hard, and it still does.

That first day in the studio, I wrote three songs. It's almost like they were waiting for me to get to Africa. I wasn't working with any African artists yet, partially because I had only thirty days to do what I usually do in six months to a year, and also because I never think of who a song might be for while I'm writing it (even if I do think about who might play on it). That's not my process. Even with "Be Like Water," I didn't think of Stevie Wonder. I always think of the song first. So when the label wanted me to pick artists, I said, "Give me a list." Writing great songs always comes first for me.

I got on the piano and just started playing the little scribbles that I always play. There was a progression I'd had in my head for a long time and I started there. In a few hours, that became "Count on Me." I had never worked so fast. Sometimes, when I work on new songs, I can get lost in the weeds. The schedule didn't allow me to do that. Instead, I needed to trust my instincts. What happens if I don't get in the way or think twice? What happens if my first idea is perfect? What if I just trust that?

I'll rise to the occasion if somebody gives me a deadline. If Netflix needs something in two weeks, I'll get it done. But that's different from PJ Morton. That's not my voice. But in Africa, it was all my voice, and the only way to do what I wanted to do was to trust myself.

What made it especially rewarding was that I hadn't written since *Watch the Sun*, two years earlier, so I guess those songs were stored up, waiting to come out. Next came "Thank You." I had always wanted to write a song that said thank you. It's such a simple concept, but that's what makes it tough to write. I started working on that idea and we were off to the races. That took a weight off me. At the end of that first day, I thought, *If this is day one of thirty, I'm okay. I don't have writer's block.*

That night, we went to a jam session that we had set up beforehand, and I ran into this jazz and gospel artist I love, Jonathan Butler. The jam session was at his manager Colin's house. We walked in and Colin already had a stage set up and great food laid out. Cape Town has a great jazz scene and some really talented people, and some local musicians were playing. There was no pressure for us to play, but the vibe was so good that we couldn't help it. We had just gotten to Africa and we were feeling good. So I did that jam session . . . and I went really hard.

Afterward, I found Jonathan and said, "Can you pop out to the studio tomorrow? I've got an idea." I played this progression that had been in my head forever but that I couldn't turn into a song. I asked, "Is there a word that you guys have that could be a refrain, a big idea?" Jonathan told me this word, *simunye*, a Zulu word that means "we are one." *Boom.* That was all I needed. I wrote the full song "Simunye" right there in twenty minutes.

The next day, I had radio and TV appearances, and then a show in Cape Town. I could feel myself overextending, and it felt like I might lose my voice, but no problem, right? I didn't realize I had an appearance in Johannesburg the next day. We did the Cape

Town show, and the sold-out audience was on fire. They knew every song and were dancing the entire time. It was so uplifting that I didn't hold anything back.

Afterward, Wade said, "You know, we've got the Mandela thing tomorrow." *Oh boy.* My voice was gone. About fifty important people, including the South African ambassador to Egypt, had paid for a private piano show at Mandela House, one of the homes Nelson Mandela had lived in. And I had nothing.

I felt terrible. But we did the appearance. I played, Tiondria sang, and then I spoke. We did a wonderful Q&A, and the people there saw that even though I couldn't sing, I was willing to give everything I had. Kortni was there, and we spent the night in Mandela's bedroom. It felt like I was where I was supposed to be.

~

We connected with people everywhere we went in South Africa, but I was there to make an album, so I had to keep working. I had time in the studio every day, no matter where we were, but I still had to do TV and radio appearances, too. Unfortunately, after the Mandela event, I had to cancel everything scheduled for the next three days so I could get my voice back. I needed my voice back for the Johannesburg show, which was also sold out.

I had fallen into a process. I was writing some chord progressions but mostly melodies, and I used the days that I had no voice to write lyrics. I was trying to use every minute I had because I didn't want to be up against the clock without a full album's worth of songs.

By the time we got to Johannesburg, I had my voice back, which was lucky, because the Johannesburg show was twice the size of the Cape Town show. I knew it was sold out before we even got to Africa, but I didn't know if they knew my songs. Was I going to have to do extra work? Were they going to sing? Were they going to move?

We pulled up to the casino where the theater was, and I saw the line of people waiting to get in, snaking down the street for hundreds of yards. That night, when we opened the backstage door, we could hear the buzzing of the crowd. When we finally went out, we opened with "Good Morning," which was playing on the radio in South Africa. Just like in Cape Town, the audience was singing every word! I felt at home once again. These were my people. I could have been back at the Apache Café in Atlanta; it was the same vibe. We were speaking the same language.

We ended the show the same way we end in the States, with "How Deep Is Your Love," and the crowd harmonized on their own, without me telling them to. We stayed in Johannesburg a little longer because I had to do *Idols SA*, their version of *American Idol*. I was the coach for the top four singers. It was fun, immersing myself in all these cultures and getting to know these countries through the people.

Next up was Lagos, the capital of Nigeria. Talk about a different vibe. It's a city of *thirty million* people. For some perspective, the entire country of South Africa is sixty million. It felt like we had left New Orleans and landed in New York. In the airport, there were thousands of people everywhere all shouting, "Move out of the way!" "Get out!" and "Wrong line!" at the same time. The misconception about Nigeria is that they are mean people, but they're not. They're just busy. They've all got somewhere to be.

We landed on October 15, which is the late Fela Kuti's birthday. He's the father of Afrobeat, and every year on his birthday,

Lagos hosts a free festival called Felabration. We landed, dropped our stuff, and headed to the festival. It was beautiful chaos. There were people, dogs, and fire everywhere. We went in the back because we were the guests of Fela's son, Femi Kuti, and his family. The family keeps the festival going in Fela's memory, which is wonderful. But what I connected with most was Afrobeat, the music that's mainly from Nigeria. Listening intently, I heard New Orleans in it, and again, I was home.

There was something about Nigeria. My people were taken from here, but when they got to New Orleans, they decided to show the people there, "This is our music." I could feel that connection. It was the same with the food in Nigeria, especially with spices. Eating it took me right back to New Orleans. I found myself thinking, *Oh, this is their version of jambalaya.* My whole trip, I was connecting the dots like that between my home and the home of my ancestors.

That night, Femi and his son, Made (pronounced "MAH-day"), did their Afrobeat thing with mad horns, percussion, and dancers. During the music, I noticed that these players were all so happy. They were performing for free—they do a free show every week— at this venue called the New Afrika Shrine, which Fela started. Anybody can go there, but no police are allowed because the law was really bad to Fela during his life. In fact, he had to move to Ghana to avoid prosecution.

(Incidentally, Ghana has its own unique music named *highlife*, which also feels strongly related to the music of New Orleans. It's said that even after Fela fled to Ghana to avoid oppression in conservative Nigerian society over his polygamy, he continued to develop his sound. What an incredible artist.)

214

You would think a place like the New Afrika Shrine might be a crazy, dangerous environment, but it's all love in there. I met many wonderful people, and that was just our first night in Lagos. I went into the studio the next day and three more new songs just poured out of me: "Smoke and Mirrors," "Who You Are," and "All the Dreamers." Ed, Brian, and I got in a room, built some old-school grooves, and we had our songs.

An album was beginning to form. I was starting to do my sequencing, seeing if these new songs would fit together on a record. When I started that, one thing that struck me was that these songs were all different styles. "Count on Me" felt like a pop song. "Simunye" sounded like a hymn. "Thank You" had an amapiano (a South African fusion genre) feel. I didn't have the luxury of time to second-guess myself. They were just good songs. Now I had to make them fit together. *Do these work? How will I transition from this one to that one?* I was working at ten times my normal pace and loving it.

We didn't have a show in Nigeria, but I met some real talent, including a young producer, P Prime, who has become one of my favorites. He came to the studio I was renting out in Lagos and played some of his beats for me. I'm not usually moved by other people's tracks, but as soon as P Prime started, I was impressed. Every one of his tracks moved me. One of those tracks became "Please Be Good," the first single off the new album.

On our last day in Lagos, I was worn out, but I accepted an invitation to visit The Cavemen—two brothers, one a bass player, one a drummer, who are both a production team and a band—at their studio. Kingsley, one of the brothers, started playing bass. I joined him on keys. His brother, Benjamin, came in on drums, and we just built this groove. I started singing the chorus right there: "Feels so good to be home again." Just like that, I had "Home Again." I wrote the verses in Egypt, but I had the chorus in a few minutes.

Even though we didn't get to perform in Nigeria, it felt most like home to me. I loved the cuisine, and the culture reminded me of New Orleans. A guy I spoke to told me that when he went to Frenchmen Street in the Marigny neighborhood, it reminded him of Lagos Island. The connection between Africa and New Orleans runs deep. Now when I'm home, I see Africa everywhere.

~

I got an awful stomach bug in Ghana. I was nauseous for my show, and I threw up backstage at the venue before we played. That might have been the hardest show I've ever had to do. The venue was beautiful, and it was packed, and I was dying. We didn't have an opening act, either, so I just put my big boy pants on and performed. The crowd loved it, but I was honestly scared to open my mouth too wide when I sang because I thought I would vomit. It was tough. I was sick for days after that. I just rested in my hotel room and wrote to one of P Prime's tracks.

But the most emotional part of the trip was going to a city called Cape Coast. That's where the boats left for the New World loaded with my ancestors who had been kidnapped from their villages. We had to drive for an hour or so from Accra, Ghana's capital, to get there. I had my whole group with me, and we were going to get a tour. I was honored to give them the opportunity, especially as Black Americans, to go back to their roots, where we all came from.

When we got to Cape Coast, we met our guide, who told us he was originally from Mount Vernon, New York. That was crazy, because when Brian and I lived in the Bronx, we used to eat breakfast at a place in Mount Vernon called the Sugar Bowl. Small world. This guy had been in Ghana for thirty years, and he took us on a tour of Cape Coast Castle.

Before we went in, our guide told us, "You're about to see how enslaved Africans were brought to the New World. You're going to see some stuff that's really heavy, so prepare your minds, take a deep breath, and get into the right mindset." Then he led us into the castle and the different caves and rooms. He also called the structure Cape Coast *Dungeon* because, he said, "While it was a castle for some, it was a prison for most."

We entered the stone room where the kidnapped people would sign away their freedom before the slave traders tore off their normal clothes and dressed them in rags. Then we walked down to the dungeons. They were horrifying: tiny, dark cells with no windows, no air circulation, and no bathrooms. I could imagine that in an African summer, the place would be sweltering and filled with disease. Our guide said there might be one hundred people at a time in a space no bigger than a modern bathroom. He told us that people would die in there but nobody would check for days. People would be locked in there with the rotting bodies.

This was the cell for the men. Then he took us to the cell for the women and children, which was just as awful. As he walked us down a tunnel where I could see out to the ocean, he told us, "This is where you would have your last free moment. You're getting out of this dungeon, but you've got to take this last walk."

He walked us through this huge gate called the Door of No Return (it even has a sign above it that reads "Door of No Return"). It felt like being in a concentration camp. The moment when we were about to walk through that gate hit me the hardest and sent chills down my spine. When they walked through that gate, that was the last time those people would ever see their families. This was the scene of the crime. I didn't even know it still existed until that moment.

We went out that gate and looked around, and then we went back in. Our guide said, "This is supposed to be the door you never returned through, but we're back here now. We survived." Heavy indeed. Cape Coast was the highlight of the whole trip for me. That was why I went.

I remembered that, back in 2019, Barack Obama had been involved with a movement called the Year of Return, in which Ghana encouraged Black people from other countries to resettle in Ghana. I loved that idea, so later I spoke with the deputy director of Ghana's Ministry of the Interior and said, "I'd be honored if you would give me dual citizenship; that would be amazing." She smiled and said, "Oh, we wouldn't be giving it to you. We would be giving it *back* to you. This was taken from your ancestors. You were taken from here. This is your right." God, that hit me hard. I'll never forget that feeling.

Next came Egypt. The rest of the band went home, leaving me, Brent, Cedric (my cameraman), Reggie, and Brian. We did things like going to an art exhibit at the pyramids. I got to see the pyramids lit up at night with nobody else around. It was breathtaking. I also went back to Johannesburg to perform on the grand series finale of *Idols SA* and close the show with "How Deep Is Your Love."

Best of all, I was done with the new album! I still had to figure out the sequences of songs and handle all the little details that I would normally be doing after six months of work, but the songs were mostly finished, including all my vocals. Later, I would add

218

horns from New Orleans so the record would be a true exchange of cultures, but the bulk of the work was done.

In early 2024, I went back to Africa with Maroon and took some time to go into the studio to mix the album. That was the first time I was able to breathe and say, "What did we just do?" I was quite emotional. Because we were filming a documentary, Cedric wanted me to talk through the whole Africa trip to sum up my thoughts and emotions. But I couldn't fully process it yet. It was too big.

We made an album and we did some terrific shows. We met some incredible musical talents. I discovered a story and a place I hadn't known existed. It was life-changing. I'm going back again, and eventually I want to bring a group of American musicians to Africa every year. We'll go from Cape Town to Cairo, which is the title of the new album and the image in the tattoo I got while I was in Africa (told you I'd come back to that eventually). Who knows what we'll find?

Chapter Sixteen

All the Dreamers

In 2024, I won another Grammy for Best Traditional R&B Performance while I was in Africa mixing *Cape Town to Cairo*, and it caught me by surprise. I ended up watching the awards show on television (in the small hours of the morning because of the time change), but Susan Carol, who performed the nominated song, "Good Morning," with me, was at the awards. She promised me that in case we won, she was ready. She said, "I've got it. I'm good. I've got my speech prepared." I told her that it feels a little different when you win, something I knew from personal experience. "You're going to say whatever comes to you," I said. She was so confident, then we won and she got up there and just cried. It was genuine and beautiful.

But Africa isn't the only dream of mine that's come true recently. In 2018, I put out a Christmas album, and on that record was a song I wrote for my daughter called "Peyton's Lullaby." Wade sent the song to Disney, and a few months later I ended up in a meeting with Tom MacDougall, president of Walt Disney

Music. He told me, "The reason I was drawn to 'Peyton's Lullaby' is because the melody is timeless." I thought, *What a concept. What if everybody decided to make something timeless?*

That was that, but I guess I was on Disney's radar, because in 2022, my friend Brandon was involved in a very hush-hush Disney project, and he told me that it had a New Orleans theme—and that they needed an original song for it. Would I be interested in getting involved? I was just coming off a crazy tour and I was exhausted, but my curiosity got the better of me. I met with Brandon, who told me that he and his team were stuck. "We were supposed to have a song by now," he said. "We don't have a song." He said he couldn't tell me more than that, and I finally lost my patience. "I don't know what you're talking about, man," I said. "I'm also tired. So you need to tell me."

Turns out Disney was shutting down the Splash Mountain rides at Disneyland and Walt Disney World and replacing them with a ride based on the movie *The Princess and the Frog*, which would be called "Tiana's Bayou Adventure." They needed a signature song for the ride, and they wanted me to see if I could write it.

Did I say I was exhausted? Not anymore. Working with Disney had been a dream of mine since the first time I saw *The Little Mermaid*. I'm a huge Disney nerd. This was my chance. I said, "I'm in. I'll do it."

The project was a continuation of Tiana's story based in 1930s New Orleans, so I started writing. I wrote three completely different songs—different sound, different keys, different rhythms, everything—and Brandon and I started sending musical ideas back and forth. The feedback was vague: *I like this, but let me give you this idea, and this is a different rhythm.* Finally, I said, "We've got to narrow this down or I'm gonna go crazy."

Now we started mixing and matching pieces from all three songs. If we liked a lyric from one, we might combine it with the chorus from the second song, and a verse from the third. It was actually a cool process, especially since I didn't have a dog in the fight. I just wanted to write something they liked. After a while, we actually had the beginnings of a song, "Special Spice," and I started building on that. The process took a whole year, in part because Disney is very strict about their lyrics. Ideas have to be expressed in a very specific way.

After that, I started working with the attraction team. This included two Black ladies, Carmen and Charita, who've been at Disney for thirty years, were in charge of the overall project, and were really excited about it. When the song was finished, they started sending it up the chain, all the way to Disney's CEO, Bob Iger, and getting feedback. It seemed like everybody loved "Special Spice"! Disney executives came down to New Orleans, and we went into the studio with some of the area's best musicians to cut that song plus music for the entire ride. It was great to see my city get its moment in the sun.

The next move was to get me to Orlando. Splash Mountain was closing in two weeks, and Disney needed to get me on the ride and walk me through the new attraction. Now things started to get even more fun. I got to Disney World, immediately went through some secret entrance, and just like that, I'm at Splash Mountain. No lines, no waiting. I thought about all the times I had been to Disney World with my kids. How nice would it have been to know about that shortcut!

The ride itself follows the same route, and it's still a flume ride, where you dive down a hill at the end and get soaked. But the story, music, characters, and overall look are totally different—different design, different animation, different story, and of course, different music. First, the team showed me a digital version of the ride, and seeing these Disney characters move to my music almost had me in tears. Next, we went through a back door and started riding Splash Mountain. During five rides, the Disney team and I talked through the various parts of the ride, listening to the song on individual headphones, and syncing up sections of "Special Spice" with specific animation and effects.

It was dope. The only problem was getting wet all five times, but I was in a good spot in the corner where I didn't get the brunt of the splash. Months later, we did a big press announcement at Preservation Hall. I am the first Black composer to have a theme song at a Disney attraction. And this is Disney, so it will be there for decades. I'll be able to take my kids and grandkids on a ride at Disneyland or Walt Disney World and tell them, "I wrote that song!"

~

Disney might be only the beginning. Netflix bought the rights to Dr. Seuss's *One Fish, Two Fish, Red Fish, Blue Fish*, and I'm writing the songs for the whole series. Scoring and writing songs for movies and TV shows is an exciting new direction for me, because I'm able to just be me. There's no pressure to make hits.

Mainstream success has had its perks, too. Back in 2022, after *Watch the Sun* came out, I had the privilege of playing the Apollo Theater in Harlem and selling it out. It was incredible to perform on the same stage that had hosted immortals like Ella Fitzgerald, Sarah Vaughan, Billie Holiday, Sammy Davis Jr., James Brown, Gladys Knight, and Luther Vandross. I played the smaller Apollo Music Café in 2017, but this was my own sold-out, headlining show. The band and I were all excited. I did my sound check and then went to record the Joe Budden podcast before the show. Then, back to the venue.

I could feel the audience's energy. New York is always electric, but there was something about doing soul and R&B music at the Apollo, which a few generations ago was often the only outlet for Black people to hear our music. Performing there felt like another dream come true. It's still one of my favorite shows to date.

Still, I'm confident that, one of these days, I'll retire. Maybe. If I do, it'll be my version of retirement, where I tour and do live shows and make a new record if and when I feel like it. The journey isn't over, but I can look back on a lot of things I'm proud of. I'm proud that I've stayed in that headspace where doing work that I love is my only requirement now. The Africa trip, *Cape Town to Cairo*, the documentary, this book—I don't do anything now that doesn't bring me joy. I'm especially proud to have paved the way for Black artists who want to go the independent route.

Other Black R&B and soul artists have told me that I gave them a blueprint and showed them there was another way to build a career without compromising. That's flattering, but I really didn't think I was revolutionizing anything. I did what I did—distribution, marketing, booking—because no one else would. I was just trying to do me, but then people started telling me, "You gave me something." I hope so.

The indie model in rock is a big thing, but it hasn't always been in Black music. Back when I was building my career, Eric Roberson and Frank McComb were two of the few Black artists who had made it as independents. I followed *their* blueprint. I like the idea that, somewhere, other musicians might be following mine.

I'm also proud to take care of the people who take care of me. Taking my band to Africa was an honor. Showing Africa to Big Ed makes me feel like I've done my duty as a friend. Ed, Brian, Jarell, Tiondria—these are my brothers and sisters, and we get to do this thing that we love together. Life doesn't get better than that.

Sometimes we'll ask each other: Did our heroes know they were living in their greatest times when they were playing live or making their best music? Did they look around, and think, *I'm here, I'm doing this, and it's a miracle*? Maybe not, especially if they were young and thought they had all the time in the world. But we do that, me and my band. Every now and then we'll say to each other, "These are the good old days. This is it; it doesn't get better than this. Let's just live. Let's just enjoy this." We want to be aware of how amazing our lives are and how lucky we are to be doing what we do.

Sometimes, I think back to the first time I played the Apollo, in 2017. Before we went on, they gave us a tour of the building, that sacred space where so many of my heroes had sung and played. That was an emotional day for me. The culture. All those ghosts. Seeing all those stars' signatures and pictures on the walls and signing my name on the wall next to all the greats. Rubbing the historic Tree of Hope that I'd seen so many artists touch through my childhood. Being in those dressing rooms. I remember taking a moment and thinking, *I'm here. I am paying attention. I am really doing this.*

I'm not ready to retire. Maybe one of these days I will. I'll be Billy Joel, Quincy Jones, or both. But not yet. I still have way too much to do.

Acknowledgments

To Kortni, my wife, for always sticking by me and supporting all my crazy ideas.

To the coolest kids—Jakai, P3, and Pey Pey, you're the reason I work so hard. You've given me my favorite job.

To my parents, for giving such an amazing foundation. Mom, thank you for your gift of thinking outside the box.

To my sisters, Jasmine and Christy, my two built-in biggest cheerleaders. Love y'all!

To Brian and Ed, for riding this music life journey with me the whole way.

To my managers. Tanya, you've been there from basically day one. I'd be lost without you. Wade, you're my brother, my sounding board, my crazy idea partner. Thanks for fighting so hard for me.

To Warryn Campbell, my big brother and mentor. Thanks for always listening and supporting.

To my uncle, Tommy Sims, another mentor who helped me see a bigger vision.

To Ernie Johnson, for always sending encouragement and love and agreeing without hesitation to write my foreword.

To my late friend Lashawn "Big Shiz" Daniels. Miss you, man.

To Sanchez Harley, for convincing my dad to get me my first studio equipment.

Acknowledgments

To my publicists, Greg and Matt at Shorefire. It has been an amazing run with you guys.

To Jennifer Smith, my literary agent, for making this book happen.

To my fans. My Day Ones! Thank you for always showing up for me! We're locked in for life.

About the Author

PJ Morton is an accomplished and dynamic entertainment executive, musician, and artist who has spearheaded global marketing plans and sold-out tours. PJ has guided his own independent boutique record label, Morton Records, to consistent success with seven consecutive years of Grammy nominations (twenty nominations and five wins). In an unprecedented feat, four of the five R&B albums released on Morton Records have garnered Best R&B Album nominations at the Grammys. In addition, he has received multiple BET, Soul Train, NAACP Image, Dove, and Stellar award nominations and wins. He has also been honored with the Bennie Award, the prestigious award from Morehouse College's Candle in the Dark Gala. Past honorees include Charles Phillips, Denzel Washington, Spike Lee, Oprah Winfrey, Henry "Hank" Aaron, Samuel L. Jackson, Muhammad Ali, and Andrew Young.